The Courageous Mindset

Transform Your Life and Work with the 5 Second Rule

Delores Paul

Table of Contents

Everyday Courage

Courage is the ability to do things that feel difficult, scary, or uncertain.

It isn't reserved for just a chosen few.

Courage is a birthright. It's inside all of us.

And it's waiting for you to discover it.

One moment of courage can change your day. One day can change your life. And one life can change the world.

That's the true power of courage; it reveals you. The greatest version of you.

Discover your courage, and you will be capable of accomplishing and experiencing anything you dream about.

Yes, even changing the world.

PART1

THE 5 SECOND RULE

CHAPTER ONE

FIVE SECONDS TO CHANGE YOUR LIFE

IF YOU'RE SEARCHING FOR

THAT ONE PERSON WHO WILL CHANGE YOUR LIFE

LOOK IN THE MIRROR

You are about to learn something remarkable—it takes just five seconds to change your life. Sounds like a gimmick, doesn't it? It's not. It's science. I'll prove it to you. You change your life one five-second decision at a time. In fact, it's the only way you change.

This is the true story of the 5 Second Rule: what it is, why it works, and how it has transformed the lives of people around the world. The Rule is easy to learn and its impact is profound. It's the secret to changing anything. Once you learn the Rule, you can start using it immediately. The Rule will help you live, love, work, and speak with greater confidence and courage every day. Use it once and it'll be there for you whenever you need it.

I created the 5 Second Rule at a time in my life when everything was falling apart. And by everything, I mean everything: my marriage, finances, career, and self-esteem were all in the gutter. My problems seemed so big that it was a struggle each morning just to get out of bed. That's actually how the Rule began—I invented the Rule to help me break my habit of hitting the snooze button.

When I used the Rule for the very first time seven years ago, I thought it was silly. Little did I know that I had invented a powerful metacognition technique that would change absolutely everything about my life, work, and sense of self.

What's happened to me since discovering the 5 Second Rule and the power of five second decisions is unbelievable. I not only woke up—I shook up my entire life. I've used this one tool to take control and improve everything from my confidence to my cash flow, my marriage to my career, and my productivity to my parenting. I have gone from bouncing checks to seven figures in the bank and from fighting with my husband to celebrating 20 years of marriage. I've cured myself of anxiety, built and sold two small businesses, been recruited to join the teams at CNN and *SUCCESS* magazine, and I'm now one of the most-booked speakers in the world. I've never felt more in control, happy, or free. I couldn't have done any of it without the Rule.

The 5 Second Rule changed everything … by teaching me just one thing: *HOW* to change.

Using the Rule, I replaced my tendency to overthink the smallest moves with a bias toward action. I used the Rule to master self-monitoring and become more present and productive. The Rule taught me how to stop doubting and start believing in myself, my ideas, and my abilities. And, the Rule has given me the inner strength to become a better and much happier person, not for others, but for me.

The Rule can do the same for you. That's why I am so excited to share it with you. In the next few chapters, you'll learn the story behind the Rule, what it is, why it works, and the compelling science to back it up. You'll discover how five second decisions and acts of everyday courage change your life. Finally, you'll learn how you can use the #5SecondRule in combination with the latest research-backed strategies to become healthier, happier, and more productive and effective at work. You'll also learn how to use it to end worry, manage anxiety, find meaning in your life and beat any fear.

And, that's not all. You'll see proof. Lots of proof. This book is packed with social media posts and first-hand accounts from people all over the world who are using the Rule to make some amazing things happen. Yes, the Rule will help you wake up on time, but what it really does is something far more remarkable—**it wakes up the inner genius, leader, rock star, athlete, artist, and change agent inside of you.**

When you first learn the Rule, you'll likely start using it to stick to your goals. You might **use the Rule to push yourself** to get to the gym like Margaret does when she isn't "feeling it."

Margaret
@MRuvoldt

Planned on the treadmill first thing today. Woke up & wasn't feeling it. Then I thought @melrobbins #5secondrule

Or you may **use the Rule to become more influential at work**. That's how Mal first used the Rule—to find the courage to meet with his boss and talk about his career goals (something that so many of us fear). Thanks to the Rule, it not only happened, but it went great:

malzakmeh @mel_robbins, today I made a huge step forward and talked to my boss about my next goal and he totally supported me #5secondrule! Thank you @mel_robbins 😊 😊

That's another thing that's unique about the Rule—I may have created it, but it's not just my story to tell. Inside this book, you'll meet people around the world from all walks of life who are using the Rule, in ways big and small, to take charge of their lives. Their diverse experiences will help you understand just how limitless the applications for the Rule and its benefits truly are.

You can use the Rule to become more productive. Before the 5 Second Rule, Laura used to make endless to-do lists and sat around making excuses and being a jerk to herself. Now, there's no room in Laura's life for excuses—only action. Laura has increased her cash flow by $4,000 a month, finished her bachelor's degree, and hiked a few 4,000 footers. Next up, run a marathon.

 Laura

I heard you speak this past winter and you told me to stop being a jerk to myself, then this happened!!! Thank you for motivating the jerk out of me!

You can use the Rule to step outside of your comfort zone and become more effective at networking. Ken used the 5 Second Rule the same day he learned it at the Project Management Institute National Conference to meet "movers and shakers," Matthew used it to cold-call C-Level executives, and Alan used it to meet "a dozen folks I wouldn't have otherwise" at a PGA Tour event.

Ken Riches @Buckoclown1
@melrobbins Really enjoyed your presentation to PMI NA LIM on Saturday. I have used the 5 second rule at least three times since!

↩   ⇄ 1   ♥ 7   • • •

Mel Robbins @melrobbins
@Buckoclown1 how did you use it?!

↩   ⇄   ♥   • • •

Ken Riches
@Buckoclown1

@melrobbins twice to introduce myself to movers and shakers, once to get up and get a bunch of work done this AM

Matthew Smith

@melrobbins emailed c-level execs on friends' behalf to get informational interviews. And THEY RESPONDED and everything. 5 sec rule wins!

Alan
@TheIdOfAlan

@melrobbins Great job at the PGA TOUR! I've already used the 5 sec. trick to meet a dozen folks I wouldn't have otherwise. #GoodStuff

You can also use the Rule to self-monitor and control your emotions. Jenna uses the Rule as a mom to practice "patience instead of snapping at" her kids. She's also using it as a sales tool in her new direct selling business. The Rule helps her stop thinking about how "intimidating" it is to sell and gives her the courage to just start selling.

 Jenna

Hi Mel!! Well I really just started putting the 5 second rule into motion. 2 areas of my life I have started really practice using it is with my kids and having the patience instead of snapping at them. I feel like it has given me the extra 5 seconds to put my thoughts together before jumping the gun. Also in building my Yoli business. I take 5 seconds and just ask, just talk to someone and bring up my my business. As u talked about it thinking about the answer rather than thinking about doing it can be very intimidating in this kind of business. Just have to use the 5 seconds and do it instead of thinking about it!! I absolutely loved hearing you in person!!! It was great! Thank you!! I plan to keep putting the 5 second rule in motion throughout many aspects of my life that I want to work on! Hope you  have a fabulous day!

Executives inside some of the world's most respected brands are using the Rule to help their managers change, drive sales, engage teams, and innovate. Take Crystal at USAA, whose entire sales team is using the 5 Second Rule and the result has been awesome—they've jumped to "#1 in our location."

Crystal

I have my whole team at USAA doing the 5 second rule so far we have jumped to #1 in our location our goal it to be the number one in the entire company! Here is one of the forms you sent me. I have more to follow.

The #5SecondRule is so easy to learn and so important for confidence that we see managers, like Muz, teaching it to their teams all over the world.

Muz
@muze63

The entire staff glued to a great #TEDtalk by @melrobbins this morning #motivation #5secondrule. Thank you, Mel :)

You'll also be inspired by the stories of people who are finding the courage to stop thinking and start putting their ideas into action. Mark, who after decades of thinking about starting a nonprofit ice hockey league for inner city kids, used the Rule to finally get the idea "out of my head" and "into action." He's now partnered with former Olympians and NHL alumni to create camps, clinics, and leagues.

I worked in around the National Hockey League for most of the 1980s and 1990s. I always thought that it was a shame that inner city kids had little access to the sport, which tends to be expensive and impractical for many families.

I always had a concept of hockey legends bringing hockey to the inner city via street hockey. Unfortunately, I put the "emergency break" on each time I had this thought and never followed through with it.

Then in 2013, I watched Mel Robbins TEDx talk and at the 19th minute of a 21-minute presentation, she introduced the "5 second rule."

Bingo!

I immediately got the inner city hockey program out of my head and put it into action. Soon, I joined forces with former US Olympic hockey Star David A. Jensen and the Boston Bruins Alumni to create the "Hockey in the Streets" program, which now conducts camps, clinics and leagues in many urban areas throughout New England.

SAs the program continues to expand, thousands of urban kids will have the chance to experience the great game of hockey. But, it couldn't have happened with the "emergency break" on!
http://www.dajhockey.com/summer-2016-urban-street-hockey-program.html

Summer 2016 Urban Street Hockey Program

The Massachusetts Department of Conservation and Recreation…

The Rule is also a powerful tool in the battles of addiction and depression. Bill learned about the #5SecondRule on a Reddit thread and it was the "Right message. Right place. Right time." He started using the Rule's "countdown trick" to quit drinking and it's working "amazing!!" He just celebrated his 40th birthday completely sober.

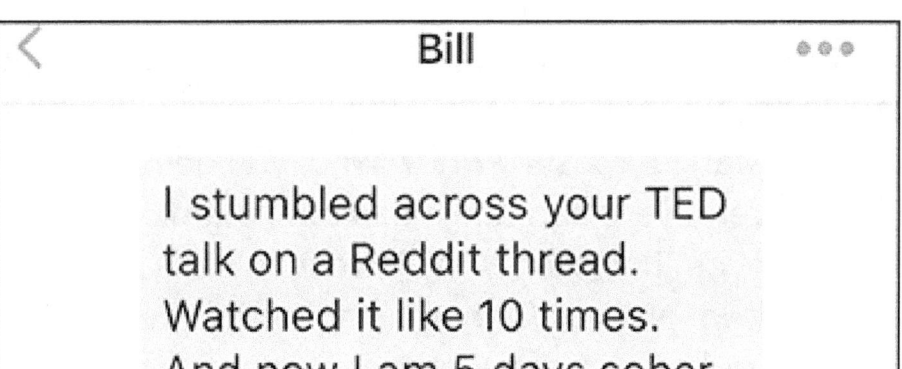

Hi Mel!! I am doing very well. I turned 40 on Saturday, and have stayed sober the entire time!!! I have been to a couple social functions and used the countdown trick, it works amazing!!

And it might even save your life A work colleague of mine recently reached out and shared a very poignant #5SecondRule story with me. After he and his wife split up, he fell into a deep depression. It got so bad that he "contemplated suicide." At his lowest point, he used the Rule to "put it down and call for help." Finding the courage to get out of his head by counting 5- 4- 3- 2- 1 and then calling for help saved his life.

> Mel, hope all is well. I have been meaning to write you for a while. As you know I have heard you speak a few times, we have hung out and I follow your various 'posts'. Know what you do matters. My wife and I split over a year ago and it has been hard. So hard that I contemplated suicide, however at my lowest point I said to myself 5-4-3-2-1 put it down and call for help. I am doing great now, life is good and I have rediscovered my purpose. Never doubt the good you are doing and the difference you are making. 5-4-3-2-1 go out and have a great day. Cheers

In using the Rule for more than seven years, and hearing from people all over the world, I've come to realize that every single day we face moments that are difficult, uncertain, and scary. Your life requires courage. And that is exactly what the Rule will help you discover—the courage to become your greatest self.

How Can One Simple Tool Work in So Many Powerful Ways?

Great question. The #5SecondRule is only ever working on one thing—YOU. You have greatness inside of you. Even at your lowest point, greatness is there. The Rule will give you both the clarity to hear that greatness and the courage to act on it.

Using the Rule, I have discovered the courage to do things that I had spent years thinking about and making excuses for. Only through action have I unlocked the power inside of me to become the person that I've always wanted to be. And the confidence I exhibit on TV, online, and on stage is what I call "Real Confidence."

I've built Real Confidence by learning how to honor my instincts with action so that they come to life in the real world. I use the word "honor" on purpose. That's what you are doing when you use the Rule. You are honoring yourself. You are championing your ideas. And each time you use it, you take one step closer to being the person you are truly meant to be. I have changed from the kind of person who just thinks about my ideas to having the confidence to share, act on, and pursue them. If you use the Rule consistently and you honor your instincts with action, the exact same transformation will happen to you.

Marlowe discovered just how easy it is to use the Rule to transform herself. Days after learning the Rule, she used it to stop thinking about signing up for classes and actually do it, which was something she "had been wanting to do but kept making excuses for, for a long time."

Marlowe

Mel!!!! I was a part of the Achievers team when you came and gave a life-changing, earth shattering talk at our ACE conference in Toronto September 14th. I just started reading your book and haven't been able to put it down. In fact, before even getting half way through it, I was reading it in bed one evening and I literally put your book down, got up and drove to York University and signed up for courses- something I had been wanting to do but kept making excuses for, for a long time. It is absolutely incredible and awe-inspiring how easy things become once you wrap your head around your own ability to PUSH yourself. I love you, and I love your book! Your wisdom needs to be shared around the world. You have truly impacted my life in such a short time and I can't even begin to describe how amazing it feels to feel in control. I sincerely hope you come out with another book soon. Sincerely- another grateful fan.

 Marlowe

People need to understand just how freaking EASY it is once you actually try it. I'm astonished really. That's why I felt the need to reach out, I know you hear these stories everyday I'm sure but I have literally been procrastinating about signing up for these last 2 courses for years- honestly. And in the middle of your book I was like, what am I waiting for? All I have to do is get in my car and drive 30 minutes to sign up and just do it. So I did. And I'm currently enrolled for this fall semester and winter and I feel challenged and it's exciting! I know that once I accomplish this I'll be looking for my next mountain to climb and I finally feel like I'm doing something for me that will benefit me and what's better is I had the PUSH to do it myself. It feels great. It was a privilege to be able to sit in on your talk, truly! You're an inspiration

As Marlowe put it, "it's absolutely incredible and awe-inspiring how easy things become once you wrap your head around your own ability to PUSH yourself."

She's right. Once you start using the Rule to push yourself out of your head and into action, you'll be "astonished" by how easy it is to make a five second decision that changes everything.

As I used the Rule more and more in my life, I realized that I was making small decisions all day long that held me back. In five seconds flat, I'd decide to stay quiet, to wait, and not to risk it. I'd have an instinct to act and within five seconds my mind would kill it with doubt, excuses, worry, or fear. **I was the problem and in five seconds, I could push myself and become the solution.** The secret to change had been right in front of my face the entire time—five seconds decisions.

Have you ever seen that famous commencement address David Foster Wallace gave at Kenyon College in 2005? If you haven't seen or read this speech, you can find it on YouTube and it's definitely worth the 20 minutes it takes to watch.

In it, Wallace steps up to the mic and starts off with this joke:

There are these two young fish swimming along, and they happen to meet an older fish swimming the other way, who nods at them and says, "Morning, boys, how's the water?"

And the two young fish swim on for a bit, and then eventually one of them looks over at the other and goes, "What the hell is water?"

You can hear the audience laugh in the video, and then Wallace explains the immediate point of the fish story is that *"the most obvious, important realities are often the ones that are the hardest to see and talk about."*

For me, the hardest thing to see and talk about was the very nature of change itself. I had always wondered why it was so damn hard to make myself do the things that I knew I should do in order to expand my career, enrich my relationships, become healthier, and improve my life. Discovering the #5SecondRule gave me the million-dollar answer—change comes down to the courage you need every day to make five second decisions.

You Are One Decision Away from a Completely Different Life

Inside this book, I'm going to share everything that I've learned about change and the power of everyday courage. You're going to love what you are about to learn. The coolest part will be when you start to use the Rule and see the results for yourself. You will not only wake up and realize just how much you've held yourself back. You will also awaken the power that's been inside of you all along.

As you read the stories inside these pages, you might even realize that you've used the #5SecondRule before. If you look back on your life and reflect on some of the most important moments, I guarantee that you've made a life-changing decision purely on instinct. In five seconds flat, you made, what I call, a "heart-first decision." You ignored your fears and let your courage and your confidence speak for you. Five seconds of courage makes all the difference.

Just ask Catherine. When she first learned about the #5SecondRule at her company's executive leadership offsite, it made her realize she had used the Rule to make one of the most important decisions of her life—she just didn't realize it at the time. In 1990, her sister Tracy was killed and Catherine traveled back home to help. That's when "a 5 Second decision" changed not only her life "but so many others as well." She decided to raise her sister's "two little ones" who were "left behind" when Tracy died.

Catherine

Hi Mel,
Can't wait for your book. Makes me
appreciate all the great things that have come
out of trusting your gut. My sister Tracy was
killed by her husband in 1990. Her two little
ones were left behind Dan 4 and Trudy 18
months. I came home to help out with the
kids........I still remember walking in that day,
never having met them and Trudy walked
right up to me and gave me a hug. A 5
second decision led to raising them, adopting
them, getting married, having a third, and
now a grandma to Trudy' 3 kids. 5 seconds
not only changes your life but so many others
as well. I finally get what a "no brainer" really
means. Your heart speaks first and you listen.
Thanks for your inspiration. I know I have a
story to tell too.
Always a FAN,
Catherine

I love how she describes the decision as a "no brainer"—because when you act with courage, your brain is not involved. Your heart speaks first and you listen. The Rule will teach you how.

Will it take some effort on your part to discover the power within you? Yes, it will. But as Marlowe said just a few pages ago, "It is absolutely incredible and awe-inspiring how easy things become" when you do.

Doing the work to improve your life is simple, you can do it, and it's work you want to do—because it's the most important work that there is. It is the work of learning how to love and trust yourself enough to stop waiting and to start leaning into all the magic, opportunity, and joy that your life, work, and relationships have to offer.

I'm so excited to hear about what happens when you start using the #5SecondRule. But I'm jumping ahead of the story. Before we can talk about all of the exciting ways that you can use the Rule, I need to take you back to 2009 and explain how this all started.

cour-age
/'kerij/

noun

- **The ability to do something that is difficult or scary**
- **Stepping outside of your comfort zone**
- **Sharing your ideas, speaking up, or showing up**
- **Standing firm in your beliefs and values**
- **And some days...getting out of bed.**

CHAPTER TWO

HOW I DISCOVERED THE 5 SECOND RULE

"COURAGE IS FOUND

IN UNLIKELY PLACES."

J.R.R. TOLKIEN

This all started in 2009. I was 41 years old and facing some major problems with money, work, and in my marriage. As soon as I woke up each morning, all I felt was dread.

Have you ever felt that way? It's the worst. The alarm rings, and you just don't feel like getting up and facing the day. Or, you lie awake at night with your head spinning as you worry about all of your problems.

That was me. For months, I felt so overwhelmed by the problems I had that I could barely get out of bed. When the alarm rang at 6 a.m., I would lie there and think about the day ahead, the lien on the house, the negative account balance, my failed career, how much I resented my husband…and then I would hit the snooze button. Not once, but over and over again.

In the beginning, it wasn't a big deal, but as is the case with any bad habit, as time went on, it snowballed into a much bigger problem that impacted my entire day. By the time I finally got up, the kids had missed the bus and I felt like I was failing at life. I spent most of my days tired, running late, and feeling totally overwhelmed.

I don't even know how it started—I just remember feeling so defeated all the time. My professional life was in the gutter. Over the past 12 years, I had changed careers so many times that I was developing multiple personalities. After graduating from law school, I started my career as a public defender for the Legal Aid Criminal Defense Society in NYC. Then I met my husband Chris and we got married and moved to Boston so that he could pursue his MBA. In Boston, I worked crazy hours for a large law firm and was miserable all the time.

When our daughter was born, I used my maternity leave to look for a new job and landed in the Boston startup scene. I worked for several tech startups during those years. It was fun and I learned a lot but I never felt like tech was the right career for me.

I hired a coach to help me figure out "what to do with my life." Working with a coach led me to want to become one. So, like a lot of people, I worked during the day, focused on the kids when I got home, and then I studied at night to get the certification I needed. Eventually, I launched a coaching business. I loved it, and I would probably still be doing it if the media had not called.

My media career began as a fluke: *Inc.* magazine published an article featuring my coaching business and an executive at CNBC saw it and called. That one call led to lots of meetings. After months of tryouts, I landed a "development deal" with ABC and a call-in radio show on Sirius.

Sounds fancy, but it wasn't. I was surprised to learn that most development deals pay next to nothing and that radio pays even less than that. In reality, I was a mother of three driving back and forth to NYC, sleeping on friends' couches in the city, coaching clients on the side to make the ends meet, leaning too much on friends and family to fill the childcare gaps, and doing whatever I could to make it all work.

After several years scraping by in the media business, I got my "big break." I was cast to host a reality show for FOX. I had visions of magically solving all of our financial problems by becoming a TV star. What a joke. We shot a few episodes of a show called *Someone's Gotta Go*, and then the network tabled the show. In an instant, my media career hit a dead end. I only got paid if we were shooting. I found myself unemployed and locked into a contract for ten months that prevented me from pursuing another media job.

By this point, Chris had finished his MBA and started a thin crust pizza restaurant with his best friend in the Boston area. In the beginning, things were going great. The first location was a home run, the company won Best of Boston™, multiple regional awards, and the pizza was fantastic. They opened up a second restaurant and, on the encouragement of a large grocery chain, a wholesale operation. On the outside, it looked like business was booming. But on the balance sheet, the wheels were starting to come off. They had expanded too quickly. The second restaurant failed and the wholesale business needed more cash to grow. Things got scary very fast.

Like a lot of small business owners, we had poured our home equity line and life savings into the restaurant business and it was now disappearing before our eyes. We had no savings left and the home equity line was fully tapped out. Weeks went by without Chris getting paid. Liens started to hit our house.

With me out of work and Chris's business struggling, the financial pressure mounted; scary letters from attorneys seemed to arrive daily and checks constantly bounced. The collection calls were so relentless that we unplugged the phone. When my dad sent us money to cover the mortgage, I was both grateful and ashamed.

In public, we tried to keep up appearances because so many friends and family members had invested in the restaurant business, which only made the pressure worse. Chris and his partner were working around-the-clock to save it. I tried to keep an upbeat façade, but on the inside I was overwhelmed, embarrassed, and afraid. Our financial problems were tearing us apart. I blamed the restaurants and he blamed me for pursuing a career in the media business. In truth, we were both to blame.

No matter how bad your life can seem, you can always make it worse. I did. I drank too much. Way too much. I was jealous of friends who didn't have to work. I was bitchy and judgmental. Our problems seemed so big that I convinced myself there was nothing I could do. Meanwhile, in public, I just pretended everything was fine.

In hindsight, I can see that is was just easier to feel sorry for myself and blame Chris and his struggling business than to take a look in the mirror and pull myself together. The best way to describe how I felt was "trapped." I felt trapped by my life and the decisions I had made. I felt trapped by our money problems. And I felt trapped in a frustrating struggle with myself.

I knew what I should or could be doing to make things better, but I couldn't make myself do those things. They were small things: getting up on time, being nicer to Chris, getting support from friends, drinking less, and taking better care of myself. But knowing what you need to do isn't enough to create a change.

I would think about exercising, but I wouldn't. I would consider calling a friend to talk, but I didn't. I knew that if I tried to find a job outside of the media industry it would help, but I couldn't motivate myself to look. I didn't feel comfortable going back to coaching people because I felt like such a failure myself.

I knew what I needed to do but I couldn't make myself take action. And that's the thing that makes changing so hard. Change requires you to do things that feel hard and scary. Change requires courage and confidence—and I was tapped out of both.

What I did do was spend a lot of time thinking. Thinking made everything worse. The more I thought about the situation that we were in, the more afraid I felt. That's what your mind does when you focus on problems—it magnifies them. The more I worried, the more uncertain and overwhelmed I became. The more I thought, the more paralyzed I felt.

Every night, I'd have a few drinks to take the edge off. I'd climb in bed drunk or buzzed, close my eyes, and dream about a different life—one where I didn't have to work and all of our problems had magically disappeared. The moment I woke up, I had to face reality: my life was a nightmare. I was 41, unemployed, in financial ruin, struggling with a drinking problem, and had zero confidence in my or my husband's abilities to fix our problems.

That's where the snooze button came in. I hit it…two, three, or four times a morning. When I hit that snooze button it was the one moment every day where I actually felt like I was in control. It was an act of defiance. It was as if I were saying,

*"Oh yeah?! Take that, life! **** you! I'm not getting up right now, I'm going back to sleep. So, there!"*

By the time I finally got up, Chris had already left for the restaurants, the kids were in various states of dress, and the school bus was long gone. To say mornings were chaotic would be putting it politely. They were a train wreck. We were always late. I forgot lunches, backpacks, gym bags, and permission slips as we raced out the door. I felt ashamed by the number of balls I dropped every single day. Feeling that shame just put me on edge even more.

And here's the kicker: I knew what I needed to do to start my day right. I needed to get up on time, make breakfast, and get the kids on the bus. Then I needed to look for a job. It's not like I had to climb Mount Everest. However, the fact that it was simple stuff actually made it worse. I had no legitimate excuse for why I couldn't get it done.

My self-confidence was in a death spiral. If I couldn't even get up on time, how the heck could I have faith in myself to fix the bigger financial and marriage problems that Chris and I faced? Looking back, I can see that I was losing hope.

Have you ever noticed how the smallest things can feel so hard? Having heard from thousands of you, I know that I am not alone on this one. The list of *hard* things is surprisingly universal:

Speaking in a meeting	Hitting "send" on emails	Stepping on a dance floor
Staying positive	Sticking to your plan	Publishing your work
Making a decision	Leaving the house	Getting to the gym
Finding time for yourself	Volunteering to go first	Eating in moderation
Asking for feedback	Showing up at a reunion	Saying "no"
Raising your hand	Blocking an ex on social media	Asking for help
Asking for a raise	Talking to someone you find attractive	Letting your guard down
Ending self-doubt		Admitting you are wrong
Working on your résumé		Listening

In my case, it was getting up on time. Lying in bed every night, I would make promises to myself that tomorrow I would change:

Tomorrow, I will change. Tomorrow, I will wake up earlier. Tomorrow, I will have a better attitude and try a little harder. I will go to the gym. I'll be nice to my husband. I'll eat healthy. I won't drink so much. Tomorrow I will be the future me!

And with that vision in mind and a heart full of hope, I'd set my alarm for 6 a.m. and close my eyes. And the cycle would begin the very next morning. As soon as that alarm rang, I didn't feel like the "future me." I felt like the old me, and the old me wanted to keep sleeping.

Yes, I thought about getting up, and then I would hesitate, roll toward the alarm, and hit the snooze button. Five seconds was all it took for me to talk myself out of it.

The reason that I didn't get out of bed was simple: I just didn't *feel like it*. I would later learn that I was stuck in what researchers call a "habit loop." I had hit the snooze button so many mornings in a row the behavior was now a closed-loop pattern encoded in my brain.

Then one night, everything changed.

I was about to turn off the TV and head to bed when a television commercial caught my attention. There on the screen was the image of a rocket launching. I could hear the famous final five-second countdown, 5- 4- 3- 2- 1, fire and smoke filled the screen, and the shuttle launched.

I thought to myself, "*That's it, I'll launch myself out of bed tomorrow…like a rocket. I'll move so fast I won't have time to talk myself out of it.*" It was just an instinct. One that I could have easily dismissed. Luckily, I didn't. I acted on it.

The fact is, I wanted to solve our problems. I didn't want to destroy my marriage or keep feeling like the world's worst mom. I wanted to be financially secure. I wanted to feel happy and proud of myself again.

And I Desperately Wanted to Change. I Just Didn't Know How.

And this is an important point in my story. This instinct to launch myself out of bed was my inner wisdom talking. Hearing it was a tipping point. Following its instructions was life-changing. Your brain and your body send you signals to wake up and to pay attention. This idea of launching myself out of bed is an example of that. Your instincts may seem stupid in the moment, but when you honor them with deliberate action, it can change your life.

There's more to this point about acting on your instincts than just the phrase "trust your gut." New research from the University of Arizona, in partnership with Cornell and Duke, has shown that there's a powerful connection between your brain and your instinct to act. When you set a goal, your brain opens up a task list. Whenever you are near things that can help you achieve those goals, your brain fires up your instincts to signal to get that goal completed. Let me give you an example.

Let's say you have a goal to get healthier. If you walk into a living room, nothing happens. If you walk past a gym, however, your prefrontal cortex lights up because you are near something related to getting healthier. As you pass the gym, you'll feel like you *should* exercise. That's an instinct reminding you of the goal. That's your inner wisdom, and it's important to pay attention to it, no matter how small or silly that instinct may seem.

Subconsciously, my brain was signaling me to pay attention to this rocket launch on TV. In that five-second moment, my brain was sending me a very clear set of instructions:

Pay attention to that rocket launch, Mel. Grab the idea. Believe in it. And do it. Don't stop and think. Don't talk yourself out of it. Launch yourself out of bed tomorrow, Mel.

That's one of the things I've learned using the #5SecondRule. When it comes to goals, dreams, and changing your life, your inner wisdom is a genius. Your goal-related impulses, urges, and instincts are there to guide you. You need to learn to bet on them. Because, as history proves, you'll never know when your greatest inspiration will strike and where that discovery will lead you if you trust yourself enough to act on it.

This is how some of the world's most useful inventions were discovered. In 1826, John Walker discovered the match while he was using a stick to stir a pot of chemicals, and when he tried to scrape a gob off the end—it ignited. He followed his instinct to try to recreate it and this is how he discovered the match. In 1941, George de Mestral invented Velcro® after noticing how easily cockleburs attached to his dog's fur. In 1974, Art Fry got the idea for the Post-It® Note because he needed a bookmark that would stay put on a page in his hymnal until Sunday's church service, but that would not damage the pages when he removed it.

That's even how the Frappuccino was born. In 1992, an assistant manager at a Starbucks in Santa Monica noticed that sales dropped whenever it was hot outside. He had an instinct to make a frozen drink and he followed it, asking for a blender, tinkering with recipes, and giving a Vice President a sample. The first Frappucino rolled out in his store a year later.

When it comes to change, goals, and dreams, you have to bet on yourself. That bet starts with hearing the instinct to change and honoring that instinct with action. I feel so thankful that I listened to my dumb idea about launching myself out of bed like a rocket because everything in my life changed as a result of it. Here's what happened:

The next morning the alarm rang at 6 a.m. and the first thing I felt was dread. It was dark. It was cold. It was winter in Boston and I did not want to wake up. I thought about the rocket launch and I immediately felt like it was stupid. Then, I did something that I had never done before—**I ignored how I felt. I didn't think. I did what needed to be done**

Instead of hitting the snooze button, I started counting.

Backwards.

5..4..3..2..1..

And then I stood up.

That was the exact moment I discovered the #5SecondRule.

The 5 Second Rule

The moment you have an **instinct** to **act on a goal** you must

5-4-3-2-1

and **physically move** or your **brain will stop** you.

CHAPTER THREE

WHAT YOU CAN EXPECT WHEN YOU USE IT

"IT MATTERS NOT WHAT SOMEONE

IS BORN, BUT WHAT THEY GROW TO BE."

J.K. ROWLING

When I used the Rule that first morning, I was as surprised as you are that something that stupid worked. Counting backwards? 5- 4- 3- 2- 1... seriously? I didn't know why it worked. I just knew it did. I had struggled for months to wake up on time and suddenly the #5SecondRule made changing my behavior simple.

Later I would learn that when you count backwards, you mentally shift the gears in your mind. You interrupt your default thinking and do what psychologists call "assert control." The counting distracts you from your excuses and focuses your mind on moving in a new direction. When you physically move instead of stopping to think, your physiology changes and your mind falls in line. In researching this book, I discovered that the Rule is (in the language of habit research) a "starting ritual" that activates the prefrontal cortex, helping to change your behavior.

The prefrontal cortex is the part of your brain that you use when you focus, change, or take deliberate actions. I knew what the prefrontal cortex was, but I would soon learn through my research about the basal ganglia, habit loops, activation energy, behavior flexibility, cognitive biases, neural plasticity, the progress principle, and locus of control. I certainly didn't realize I had just discovered a singular technique that impacted all of them.

I used the Rule the next morning, and it worked again. And then a funny thing happened: I started to see five-second moments all day long, just like my struggle to wake up on time. If I stopped to think about what I knew I needed to do, I was toast. It took less than five seconds for excuses to flood my mind and for my own brain to stop me.

As you use the Rule, you'll see it too—there is a five-second window between your initial instinct to act and your brain stopping you. Seeing the five-second window changed everything for me. The problem was very clear. It was me. I was holding myself back, five seconds at a time.

So I made myself a simple promise: If I knew that I should do something that could change me for the better, then I would use the Rule to push myself to do it, *regardless of how I felt*. I started using the Rule to force myself to not only get up early, but also to get to the gym, look for a job, drink less, and be a better parent and wife.

> If I started to feel too tired to exercise, I would
>> 5- 4- 3- 2- 1 and push myself out the door for a run.
>
> If I started pouring a drink that I shouldn't have, I'd
>> 5- 4- 3- 2- 1 and put down the bottle of bourbon and walk away.

If I felt myself being bitchy with Chris, I'd

    5- 4- 3- 2- 1 and correct my tone and make myself be kinder.

If I caught myself procrastinating, I'd

    5- 4- 3- 2- 1 and sit down and start working on my résumé.

What I discovered is powerful: pushing yourself to take simple actions creates a chain reaction in your confidence and your productivity. By pushing yourself to take the simple steps of moving your life forward, you create momentum and experience a sense of freedom and power that's hard to accurately describe. Rachel found that the "simple step" of getting up on time "started a chain of events" that led to her losing "30 pounds, bought my first home, and reinvigorated my marriage."

From: Rachel

Message Body:
You've helped me change my life and we've never even met. Since watching your Ted Talk a few months ago I've lost 30 pounds, bought my first home, and reinvigorated my marriage. I have no idea if you'll actually see this (I imagine you get a lot of mail), but I needed to thank you for the simple challenge of getting up 30 minutes earlier. That simple step started a chain of events that have made all the difference for me.

Rachel used the word "reinvigorated," and that's exactly what the Rule does. Rebecca had the same experience. By using the Rule to 5- 4- 3- 2- 1 and push herself to make small moves forward, she's breaking out of a mental jail. No longer trapped by analysis paralysis, Rebecca feels "FREE for the 1st time in 47 years!"

Rebecca

I finally feel FREE for the 1st time in 47yrs!!!!

For the 1st time I BELIEVE IN ME....for the 1st time I LOVE ME!

There's an important concept in psychology put forth by Julian Rotter in 1954. It's called "locus of control." The more that you believe that you are in control of your life, your actions and your future, the happier and more successful you'll be. There's one thing that is guaranteed to increase your feelings of control over your life: a bias toward action.

Forget motivation; it's a myth. I don't know when we all bought into the idea that in order to change you must "feel" eager or "feel" motivated to act. It's complete garbage. The moment it's time to assert yourself, you will not feel motivated. In fact, you won't feel like doing anything at all. If you want to improve your life, you'll need to get off your rear end and kick your own butt. In my world, I call that the power of a push.

One of the reasons why the #5SecondRule is so empowering is because it turns you into the kind of person who operates with a bias toward action. If you tend to overthink every move, you'll discover the energy and confidence to stop thinking and actually move. Using the Rule strengthens your belief that you *do* have the ability to control your own fate—because you are proving it to yourself one push at a time.

Jenney is finally taking control of her health. She realized that when she would eat a meal of "canned raviolis, a bag of chips, and a soda…then complain about being overweight," she was sabotaging her efforts to lose weight. By committing to "5- 4- 3- 2- 1-HEALTHY," Jenney was able to use the Rule to give herself the "kick in the arse" she needed.

I already started this morning! My alarm clock went off this morning and I hit snooze, THEN said, "5-4-3-2-1 GO!" and got out of bed.
I had to stop at the store for lunch on my way to work. I normally get canned raviolis, a bag of chips, and a soda...then complain about being overweight. Right before I walked in the store, I said, "5-4-3-2-1 HEALTHY" and got a sandwich and a water.

I need to lose 90 to 100 pounds and starting TODAY I am going to do it! I am not going to wait till...the first day of the month, the last day of the month, Monday, Friday, or whatever future date I tell myself will work. I am starting TODAY and I want to thank YOU for being my motivation/kick in the arse I needed!

When Donna first learned the Rule at an Aveda Institute Conference she thought, "Yeah, yeah I'll use it, but it's not going to be life changing…" That's how I felt about the Rule too—that I'd just use it as a trick to beat the snooze alarm. Boy, was I wrong! So was Donna; it changed just about everything in her life and business. As Donna found, "Only we can hold ourselves back. It's amazing to see how horribly I held myself hostage out of fear and where I am today. More importantly, where I see myself in years to come."

 Donna

While still a student at the Aveda Institute Tallahassee I sacrificed many things in order to afford a ticket and travel to "Serious Business" in New Orleans. Those choices and determination changed my life in a dramatic way.

At "Serious Business" I heard incredible speakers that inspired me right at the transition point of my career. Mel spoke about the 5 Second Rule and at the time I thought yeah yeah I'll use it but it's not going to be life changing. I slowly started using it in small daily tasks: "I want to stay in bed... ugh ok 5-4-3-2-1" and I would get up and start my day. Then it subconsciously became a habit. It built confidence within me I didn't know I had.

*My boss/mentor asked me to be a salon mentor. I was one of the newest in the salons yet I was given to opportunity to coach on new products to our team members. 5-4-3-2-1-Go! Coach with confidence.

*I want to be an Aveda educator and instead of waiting on the opportunity to take classes I made that opportunity a reality. I asked my boss/mentor for a meeting to discuss to possibility and now I'm on the track for taking classes and making my dream a reality. 5-4-3-2-1-Go! Don't be afraid to ask the universe for what you want in life.

*At "Dare to Dream" an Aveda conference while sitting in the audience I thought I was covering my eyes from the stage lights when the speakers on stage thought I volunteered to speak in front of the entire venue. When they brought me the microphone I panicked for a moment. 5-4-3-2-1-Go! Be brave. Don't say no to opportunities even if you blindly stumbled upon them.

5-4-3-2-1-Go! Whatever I'm faced with - just go. My career has become so much more with making myself step off the ledge boldly. Even though in the beginning I felt like I tripped over the edge or praying someone would help pull me over. I've realized the more times I step boldly and didn't say no to opportunities the more my confidence is built and the easier it is to say yes to my future. Only we can hold ourselves back. It's amazing to see how horribly I held myself hostage out of fear and where I am today. More importantly where I see myself in the years to come. Go! Do! Say yes in... 5-4-3-2-1.

"If you're going to doubt something, doubt your limits." -Mel Robbins.

As you use the Rule more and more, you'll begin to feel courage, confidence, pride, and a sense of control. The Rule has that effect. I often tell people "the Rule will haunt you," and I mean it—just ask Darryl.

Darryl

@melrobbins My life is moving forward because of #5secondrule. You haunt my every day, in a really good way!

That's because you'll realize you've been sleepwalking through life for a long time. Something this simple, easy, and effective is also contagious. Crystal has already started using it with her son:

Crystal

I really enjoyed your presentation at Get Real 2016! So much energy and vibrancy. I am already teaching 5 4 3 2 1 Go to my 8 year old. So looking forward to seeing my life change... for the better.

The first person I told about the Rule was my husband. Chris had definitely noticed the changes, in particular that my bitchy demeanor was melting and that I was actually being proactive. It didn't take much to convince him that there was a "secret weapon" mentality he was living without.

He adopted the Rule and used it to make some major changes. He quit drinking, started meditating daily, and exercising every morning. The Rule doesn't make these things easy; it makes them happen. That's why I describe it as a tool.

Instead of avoiding the creditor calls and bankruptcy letters, we 5- 4- 3- 2- 1 to hit it head on. I used 5- 4- 3- 2- 1 to push myself to reach out to old coaching clients to rev up the referral engine. I used 5- 4- 3- 2- 1 to propel myself to go on interviews for radio hosting gigs, despite the contract issues with FOX. Together we 5- 4- 3- 2- 1 to push ourselves to meet with accountants and financial advisors to restructured our debt and do the nauseating work to face the hole we had dug, and get disciplined about slowly crawling our way out of it.

Chris brought the Rule into his business to push himself through fear, guilt, and uncertainty. He and his partner met with dozens of advisors, crunched financial models, worked day and night until they closed the wholesale business, and grew their retail locations enabling them to sell off select locations and pay back as many investors and creditors that they could. It's remarkable what Chris and Jonathan did. Grit, hustle, and commitment. They pushed, pushed, and pushed some more.

To this day, when Chris reflects on the restaurant days, his mind will sometimes drift toward feeling like a failure. When he catches himself thinking those negative thoughts, he uses 5- 4- 3- 2- 1 to redirect his mind to think about what they did build: seven restaurants, an incredible employee culture, millions in revenue, and a remarkable brand. Did it end up how he had dreamt? No, it didn't. But what he learned about business, partnership, and himself during the process is worth more than money can buy.

There's nothing more powerful than the feeling of confidence and pride you gain when you keep trudging forward, face life's challenges head on, and push yourself to change for the better. As Chris put it, "the Rule helped me process the experience of succeeding and failing—on so many levels. Ultimately, this awareness gave me power and control over my positive and negative thoughts."

As we started to reconnect with friends, the Rule would often come up. You'll find that too. Jennifer learned the Rule and told her nurse about it. Her nurse's response? "You have no idea how many times I'll need to do this a day."

Jennifer

I was talking to my nurse about my amazing trip to Nashville and was telling her about Mel Robbins 5-4-3-2-1 rule and she was blown away and going to start doing it. She said "you have no idea how many times I'll need to do this in a day." #54321 #justdoit #besomeonescheerleader #inspire #conqueryourfears

The Rule ignites something powerful in everyone who tries it. One of our friends had the courage to ask for a divorce and another left his consulting job for one that didn't require travel. A work pal lost 73 pounds and my uncle stopped talking about giving up smoking and finally quit. A friend of Chris's moved back to Maine and used the Rule to negotiate an awesome job working remotely.

The #5SecondRule gave them all what it had given me: the framework, the courage, and the method for HOW to push yourself to change.

The first time I shared the Rule in public was in 2011 during a TEDx Talk entitled *"How to Stop Screwing Yourself Over."* The funny thing is that the talk was mostly about my dream (back then) of becoming a top talk radio show host and how I help people live the lives that they really want. I only mention the #5SecondRule at the very end of the speech, and I barely even explain it. What happened next was crazy. The talk went viral. Millions of people watched it online. And that's not all. They started writing.

Every single day, I hear from people around the world who are using the Rule, just like Mark. Mark is using it to create some pretty incredible changes in just 6 months:

> **fujfocus** Just so you know, with the help of 5SR and your inspiration, I'm doing so much in the last six months, like on pace to double my business in two years, writing a book on business sale and then another one on 100 days outside of my comfort zone, finding and being with the woman beyond my dreams @amyazzarito, being closer with my kids than ever. and making plans to explore the world.

It's the coolest thing. More than 100,000 people in more than 80 countries, to date, have written to me about their experiences using it. As more and more people started to write with questions and requests for more information, I began to research the Rule in depth so that I could better explain the many ways you can use it and prove why it works. I'm a lawyer by profession, so I really went nuts on the research. I looked for precedent, evidence, and guidance as if I were going to have to prove my case about the #5SecondRule to a jury.

It took me almost three years. I read everything I could find on the subject of change, happiness, habits, motivation, and human behavior. I read social science experiments, happiness research, books on the brain, and neuroscience studies. I didn't limit my research to the "experts;" I sent questionnaires to everyday people, like you and me, who were using the Rule. Then I got on the phone, Skype, and

Google Chat, and dug into the step-by-step experiences of what someone faces the moment they choose to change.

As I deconstructed the moment of change, I uncovered something fundamental about how each and every one of us is wired. Right before we're about to do something that feels difficult, scary or uncertain, we hesitate. Hesitation is the kiss of death. You might hesitate for a just nanosecond, but that's all it takes. That one small hesitation triggers a mental system that's designed to stop you. And it happens in less than—you guessed it—five seconds.

Ever notice how fast fear and self-doubt take over your head and you start making up excuses for why you shouldn't say something or do something? We hold ourselves back in the smallest, most mundane moments every day, and that impacts everything. If you break this habit of hesitating and you find the courage to "take some kind of action," you'll be astonished by how fast your life changes. That's what Keith discovered after learning the Rule at a RE/MAX convention. Now he's able to "do extraordinary things."

 Keith Pike Mel, I first heard of you in 2015. Then I had the pleasure of seeing you live at the RE/MAX convention in Las Vegas in February 2016. You've inspired me to be able to do extraordinary things. I just had to get out of my own way and take action. In 18 months, I have achieved unbelievable success by opening 3 offices and recruiting more than 50 agents in lil ole Arkansas. No more hesitation, no more procrastination. I take some kind of action and it helps launch me to my goal. A large task suddenly becomes manageable. The hardest part is starting. Thank you, for sharing your story and for encouraging us to be the best versions of ourselves.

You see, it's not the big moves that define our lives; it's the smallest ones. Within five seconds of stopping to think, you'll have decided not to take any action on those small things. Over time, those small decisions build. And here's the kicker: We've repeated this pattern of hesitating, worrying, and doubting ourselves so much, that these actions are now habits that have encoded in our brains.

The fact that hesitating, holding yourself back, and overthinking are habits is good news. There's a simple, proven way to break or replace bad habits and the #5SecondRule is the easiest way to do it. Once you read about habit loops, starting rituals, activation energy, and the role that feelings play in triggering your decisions, you'll appreciate the magnitude of the #5SecondRule. As you use the Rule, you'll see how change hinges on five second decisions and just how easily you can take back control.

The Rule will work every time you use it. But you have to use it. It is a tool. If you stop using it, fear and uncertainty will creep back in and take control of your decisions. If that happens, just start using the Rule again.

As you use the Rule over time, you'll experience a shift inside yourself that is much deeper, a transformation that impacts confidence and inner strength. You will come face to face with the excuses, habits, feelings, insecurities, and fears that have haunted you for years. You will see the bullshit you put yourself through every day and how much precious time you waste waiting for things to change.

By using the Rule, that waiting will end. You will be absolutely amazed by how much joy and freedom you feel by making five-second decisions. Freedom is exactly how Robin described what she gets from using the Rule.

 **Robin**

@melrobbins thx 4 the life-changing #5SecondRule there is freedom in taking action.

 **Robin**

@melrobbins my passion & vision 4 making a difference R huge my confidence sometimes lags. When in doubt I apply #5SecondRule #BizPridePiper

And that's what I've gained too—life-changing freedom. The person I was seven years ago ... is gone. And that's a good thing. Every phase of your life and career will require a different you. Using the Rule, you'll become the person you're meant to become in this next phase of your life.

So, what do you say we dig into the basics of the Rule so you can start using it?

 **Mel Robbins** ✔
@melrobbins

Knowing what you need to do to improve your life takes wisdom. Pushing yourself to do it takes courage. #5SecondRule

CHAPTER FOUR

WHY THE RULE WORKS

"YOU CAN CHOOSE COURAGE OR YOU

CAN CHOOSE COMFORT, BUT YOU CANNOT HAVE BOTH."

BRENÉ BROWN

Over the years, I've received lots of questions about the #5SecondRule. I wanted to start your introduction to using the Rule by answering some of the most frequently asked question I've received about this awesome tool.

What Exactly Is the #5SecondRule?

The Rule is a simple, research-backed metacognition tool that creates immediate and lasting behavior change. Metacognition, by the way, is just a fancy word for any technique that allows you to beat your brain in order to accomplish your greater goals.

How Do I Use the Rule?

Using the Rule is simple. Whenever you feel an instinct fire up to act on a goal or a commitment, or the moment you feel that yourself hesitate on doing something and you know you *should* do, use the Rule.

Start by counting backwards to yourself: 5- 4- 3- 2- 1. The counting will help you focus on the goal or commitment and distract you from the worries, thoughts, and fears in your mind. As soon as you reach "1," move. That's it. It's so simple but let me hammer this home one more time. Anytime there's something *you know you should do*, but you feel uncertain, afraid, or overwhelmed…just take control by counting backwards 5- 4- 3- 2- 1. That'll quiet your mind. Then, move when you get to "1."

Counting and moving are actions. By teaching yourself to take action when normally you'd stop yourself by thinking, you can create remarkable change. Counting backwards does a few important things simultaneously: It distracts you from your worries, it focuses your attention on what you need to do, it prompts you to act, and it interrupts the habits of hesitating, overthinking, and holding yourself back.

If you are wondering if the Rule works if you count forward 1- 2- 3- 4- 5, instead of backwards 5- 4- 3- 2- 1, the answer is no—it doesn't. Just ask Trent.

 Trent Kruessel

Mel,

Pertaining to the 5 second rule, I've also found that it doesn't work if I count from 1 to 5. If I do that, I am tempted to say "6" and then the action is stalled. I have to count down from 5 to 1 because the next word in my mind (after 1) is "BLASTOFF". And that is definitely an action word.

Just my take.

As Trent discovered, if you count up, you can keep counting. When you count backwards 5- 4- 3- 2…there is nowhere to go after you reach "1," so it is a prompt to move.

Why Is It Called the #5SecondRule?

I get this question a lot. And I wish I had a better answer. I called it the "#5SecondRule" because that's the first thing that popped into my mind the morning I first used it, and this nam stuck. Remember, I had seen a rocket launch the night before and thought to myself, "I'll just launch myself out of bed—like a rocket!" The next morning, I counted backwards 5- 4- 3- 2- 1—because that's what NASA does when it launches a spaceship. I started with 5 for no particular reason other than it felt like the right amount of time to give myself.

I've come to learn that there are a lot of other "5 second rules" in the world, like the one about eating food off the floor, the five-second shot clock in basketball, the game Ellen DeGeneres plays on her talk show, and the five-second test you can do to see if a sidewalk's surface is too hot for your dog to walk on.

Had I known my Rule would spread around the world, I might have come up with a more original name. But in hindsight, all these #5SecondRules have something in common. They require you to physically move within a five-second window.

Physical movement is the most important part of my Rule, too, because when you move your physiology changes and your mind follows. Perhaps the name is not only apropos—it's actually perfect because it references other five-second windows in life, and that makes the Rule feel that much more familiar, universal, and true.

The Rule Sounds Like Nike's Tagline "Just Do It"...

The difference between "Just Do It" and the #5SecondRule is simple. "Just Do It" is a concept—it's *what* you need to do. The #5SecondRule is a tool—it's *how* you make yourself do it.

There's a reason why "Just Do It" is the most famous tagline in the world and resonates across all cultures. Do you know what makes the tagline so powerful? It's the word "JUST."

The word JUST is in there because Nike recognizes something we've talked a lot about in this book—right before we act, we first stop and think. "Just Do It" acknowledges that we're all struggling to push ourselves to be better and do better. We all hesitate and wrestle with our feelings before we jump in. The word JUST tells us that we're not alone. Every single one of us has these small hesitations.

It's the moment right before you ask to join the pick-up game that's already underway, the moment you contemplate whether to do a third set of reps, or when you start to question whether you'll head out the door for a run in the pouring rain.

The tagline acknowledges that you have excuses and fears and Nike is encouraging you to be bigger than them. *Come on…don't think about it…JUST DO IT. I know you're tired…JUST DO IT. I know you are afraid…JUST DO IT.*

Nike's tagline is pushing you to move past that doubt and get in the game. Nike knows that there's greatness inside of you, and it's on the other side of your excuses. It resonates profoundly because every single one of us, even an Olympic athlete, needs a PUSH. And that's where the #5SecondRule comes in; the Rule is *how* you push yourself when no coach, competitor, parent, screaming fan, or teammate is there to push you. With the Rule, you just 5- 4- 3- 2- 1 to push yourself.

Is There a Five-Second Window of Opportunity for Everyone?

Yes. There is a window for everyone between the moment you have an instinct to change and your mind killing that instinct. While your mind starts working against you in nanoseconds, the barrage of thoughts and excuses don't seem to kick into full force and stop you for a few seconds. The five-second window seems to work for everyone.

That said, by all means play around with it to make it work for you. Personally, I notice that the longer I wait between my initial impulse to act and physically moving, the louder that the excuses get, and the harder it becomes to force myself to move. As Angela found, those five-second decisions "turned into 50 seconds and then 500 seconds when the fear was deeper." She now treats the #5SecondRule as if her brain will "self-destruct" at zero:

 Angela Rae Hughes I was there and I have to thank you for that speech. I am back at home now in Seattle and want you to know that YOU moved me to take action on something I have been procrastinating because of deep self doubt and fear of failure. I had the realization that I have always used the 5-second rule in my life without recognizing it... But I also realized that those 5 seconds turned into 50 seconds and then 500 seconds when the fear was deeper. You taught me that my brain will shut it down after 5-seconds so now I have decided to treat the 5-second rule as if it will 'self destruct' (for lack of a better explanation) at zero so I better MAKE THAT MOVE! Thank you kindly, Mel Robbins, for your wisdom.

If it works for you to shorten or lengthen the window, personalize the Rule to make it work for you.

Matt, a good friend of my husband and myself, was training for his first Tough Mudder race. He lives in New Jersey and he sent this text to my husband during the freezing cold winter. He had shrunk the window to three seconds because he noticed how fast his mind would go to work to stop him.

"Tell your girlfriend Mel that the 5 second rule is working over here. I have it down to three seconds. Why contemplate life's complexities when you can be moving ahead after just 3 seconds. In 5 seconds I can make up at least 2 excuses in my mind. In three seconds my mind has already pushed the first button on my phone to move the ball ahead. As I awoke this morning I mistakenly checked the thermometer (that took 2 seconds, but in that third second I started to put on my right sneaker."

That is how the system in your brain works—the longer that you think about something, the lower your urge to act becomes. We are amazing at fooling ourselves into staying exactly where we are. As soon as that impulse to act kicks in, you start rationalizing it away. That's why you've got to move faster—so you can break free of your excuses before your mind traps you.

What Can I Use It For?

Over the years, we've heard thousands of examples of how people are using the Rule to improve their life, relationships, happiness, and work. But every example falls into one of three distinct categories for how you can use it.

• You Can Use It to Change Your Behavior

You can use the Rule to push yourself to create new habits, pull yourself away from destructive habits, and master the skills of self-monitoring and self-control so that you can be more intentional and effective in your relationships with yourself and others.

• You Can Use It to Act with Everyday Courage

You can use the Rule to discover the courage you need to do things that are new, scary, or uncertain. The Rule will quiet your self-doubt and build confidence as you push yourself to pursue your passions, share your ideas at work, volunteer for projects that stretch you, create your art, and become a better leader.

• You Can Use It to Control Your Mind

You can use the Rule to stop the barrage of negative thoughts and endless worries that weigh you down. You can also break the habit of anxiety and beat any fear. When you take control of your mind, you'll be able to think about things that bring you joy instead of focusing on the negative. And that, in my opinion, is the most powerful way to use the Rule.

Why Does Something So Simple Work?

The Rule works because it is so simple. There are all kinds of tricky ways your brain kills your urge to act. Some of my most favorite researchers, professors, and thinkers have written bestsellers and delivered epic TED Talks detailing how our own minds betray us with a seemingly endless list of tricks including cognitive biases, the paradox of choice, the psychological immune system, and the spotlight effect. What all these great researchers have taught me is that the moment you want to change, break a habit, or do something hard or scary, your brain goes to work to stop you.

Basically, your mind tricks you into thinking things through. And the moment you get tricked into doing this, you'll get trapped by your thoughts. Your mind has a million ways to talk you out of acting. That's the neurological reason why it's so hard to change. As I mentioned in Chapter One, change requires you to do things that are uncertain, scary, or new. Your brain, by design, will not let you do such things. Your brain is afraid of things that feel uncertain, scary, or new, so it will do whatever it can to talk you out of doing those things. It is part of your hard-wiring, and this hesitation happens really fast. That is why you have to act even faster to beat it.

The Rule leverages and is an example of some powerful and proven principles in modern psychology: a bias toward action, internal locus of control, behavioral flexibility, the progress principle, starting rituals, the Golden Rule of Habits, authentic pride, deliberate action, "If-Then planning," and activation energy. Throughout this book, you'll learn more about these principles as we go into greater detail about how you can use the Rule in specific areas of your life.

How Can One Rule Work On So Many Areas of My Life?

The #5SecondRule actually only works on one thing—*you*. You stop yourself from changing the exact same way every single time—you hesitate, then you overthink, and you lock yourself in mental jail.

That moment of hesitation is a killer. Hesitation sends a stress signal to your brain. It's a red flag that signals something's wrong—and your brain is goes into protection mode. This is how we are wired to fail. Think about this for a minute.

You don't hesitate all time. For example, you don't hesitate when you pour a cup of coffee in the morning. You don't hesitate when you put on your jeans. You don't hesitate when you turn on the television. You don't hesitate to call your best friend. You don't think at all. You just have the instinct to call your friend, and you pick up the phone, and you call them. But when you hesitate just before making a sales call or texting someone back, it makes your brain think that something must be wrong. The longer you think about that sales call, the less likely you'll make it.

Most of us don't even realize how often we hesitate because we've done it so often that it's become a habit. Here's how Tim described it after using the Rule:

"Honestly, I think the Rule is powerful simply because keeping it on the tip of your thoughts allows you to process and start on activities you would normally gloss over and ignore. I also keep saying, "What the hell, I'm leaning into this." So, it is powerful because it helps you break the formally embedded thought patterns about doing things and allows (me anyway) to safely 'go for it'. Seriously, why was I afraid of doing some of the things I am now doing? It was never like anything I did or didn't do was going to end the world."

But what you will soon learn is that moment of hesitation can also be used to your advantage. Every time you catch yourself hesitating, it is a push moment! The five-second window is opened and it is time to 5- 4- 3- 2- 1 to push yourself forward and be bigger than your excuses.

Seeing the 5- 4- 3- 2- 1 countdown can serve as a vivid reminder of the Rule and its importance. Art hung the numbers on his office wall to keep him motivated and moving forward all day at work:

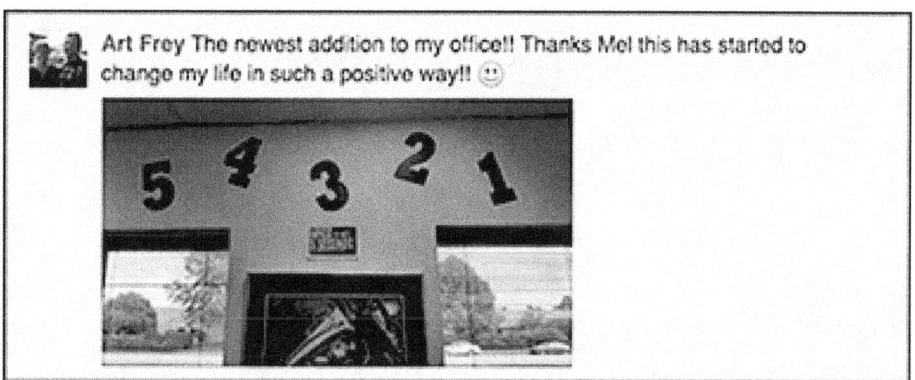

Can the Rule Create Lasting Behavior Change Too?

The Rule will beat the brain's operating system to help you win the battle with resistance in the moment. But do you know what else? Over time, as you repeat the Rule, you destroy that system all together. One thing most of us don't realize is that patterns of thinking like worrying, self-doubt, and fear are all just habits—and you repeat these thought patterns without even realizing it. If everything you do to sabotage your happiness is a habit, that means you can follow the latest research to break the habits of:

Waiting

Doubting

Holding back

Staying silent

Feeling insecure

Avoiding

Worry

Overthinking

There is a "Golden Rule of Habits" and it is very simple: In order to change any bad habit, you must replace the behavior pattern that you repeat. I will explain this in detail in Part 4 of the book. I'll teach you how to end the mental habits of worrying, anxiety, panic, and fear using the #5SecondRule in combination with all the latest research.

For now, what you need to know is this—the #5SecondRule and its countdown trick, 5- 4- 3- 2- 1- GO, will become your new behavior pattern. Instead of holding back, you'll 5- 4- 3- 2- 1 to push forward. The countdown is also what researchers call a "starting ritual." Starting rituals interrupt your bad default patterns and trigger new, positive patterns.

If you master the Rule you will reprogram your mind. You will teach yourself new behavior patterns. Instead of defaulting to worry, hesitation, and fear, you will find yourself automatically acting with courage. Over time, as you take more and more steps forward, you'll discover something else—real confidence and pride in yourself. The authentic kind that comes when you honor your goals and accomplish small wins that are important to you.

Everything that you think might be set in stone, including your habits, mindset, and personality are flexible. The implications of this for your life are absolutely thrilling. You can change your "default" mental settings and your habits one five-second decision at a time. Those small decisions add up to major changes in who you are, what you feel, and how you live.

Change your decisions and you'll change your life. And what will change your decisions more than anything? Courage.

If you have the courage to start, you have the courage to succeed.

PART2
THE POWER OF COURAGE

CHAPTER FIVE

EVERYDAY COURAGE

"I HAVE LEARNED OVER THE YEARS

THAT WHEN ONE'S MIND IS MADE, THIS DIMINISHES

FEAR; KNOWING WHAT MUST BE DONE DOES AWAY WITH FEAR."

ROSA PARKS

Before I discovered the #5SecondRule, if you had asked me to give you examples of courage, I would have given you a list of history makers. I would never have said that courage is what it takes some days to get out of bed, speak to your boss, pick up the phone, or step on a scale. I would have told you that courage is a word used to describe acts of huge bravery.

Courageous people, in my view, were the Nobel Prize winners Malala Yousafzai, Leymah Gbowee, the Dalai Lama, Aung San Suu Kyi, Nelson Mandela, and Elie Wiesel. I would have thought about Winston Churchill and Britain standing up to fight against Nazi Germany, Rosa Parks standing up for her right to keep her seat on the bus, and Muhammad Ali steadfast in his religious beliefs and refusing to fight in Vietnam. I would have been reminded of Helen Keller, who triumphed over her own disabilities to advance the rights of others; of Sir Ernest Shackleton, who overcame shocking odds to rescue the crew of the *Endurance*; or of Galileo, who challenged the Orthodox Church to advance science.

But after using the Rule for seven years and hearing from so many people around the world, I have learned a very important certainty: Everyday life is full of moments that are scary, uncertain, and difficult. Facing these moments and unlocking the opportunity, magic, and joy in your life requires tremendous courage.

Courage is precisely what the #5SecondRule gives you. The Rule gave Jose the courage to believe in his value and ask for a raise.

ibelieveinjose I made a choice in 5 seconds or less; To talk to my boss about my raise that i much deserved. I was determined I would let him know how much I'm worth. I got A 2 dollar raise.

Once he asked for one and got it, and there was a surprise waiting in his next paycheck—a bigger one.

Unexpected Love! What a great shout out. Thank you very much. I love you too. My currency holders surprised me a week later. When I looked at my check they added a dollar. Making a total of a 3 dollar raise! I was surprised. I thought of what he said during our conversation, "You're too valuable", with no hesitation he agreed on the $2 I asked for. Reading and philosophy has given me courage and balance. Again thank you very much. Best of luck! I am here if you ever need me. Your friend, Jose

The Rule gave Bryce the courage to put two years into writing and publishing a cookbook. And he didn't stop there. He got Barnes and Noble to host a book signing. As Bryce puts it, "you can achieve anything that you are passionate about and are willing to work for."

brycepalmyra

brycepalmyra After two years of dedication and hard work, I published my first cookbook, Things to Bring My Family When I Die; but, I wanted to push myself a little further. I wanted to tell life-coach, motivator, and CNN legal analysis, Mel Robbins, about it. Seconds later I started writing an email that would change my life. You're an incredible, Mel. The world needs more people like you who teach us to reach for the stars. #5SecondRule

What's even cooler? Bryce was only 15 at the time!

The Rule helped Martin push through nine years of "one excuse after another" and slamming "on those brakes hard" to go back to school and pursue a second master's degree that will give him a more fulfilling career.

> Subject: TedX: How to Stop Screwing Yourself Over
>
> Message: Hi Mel,
>
> I have watched your TedX presentation earlier this evening and found it to be funny, enlightening and most of all it gave me a lot of food for thought.
>
> Having suffered with depression and anxiety issues since graduating University in my 30's I have slammed on those breaks hard for the last 9 years coming up with one excuse after another not to go on and peruse a Masters degree and have since been stuck in basic administration roles.
>
> I have taken your advice, dug my old course books out so I can brush up on my previous studies and have started looking online for a suitable Masters degree.
>
> Thank you for giving me the kick up the arse I needed. I know I'm just at the bottom of the mountain and I am just taking my first steps and know I'll stumble, but I now know that there inspirational people like yourself I can refer back to to get my moving again.
>
> Many thanks.

Juanita learned to listen to her inner wisdom. Instead of "thinking" about a job search and a company her friend recommended, she picked up the phone and called "right now"—and guess what she got? Exactly what she pushed herself to go and get—a dream job.

Juanita
View Profile

5 second rule story- I've been doing a lot of soul searching, looking for a new job, asking myself what did i want - i stopped telling myself i was fine with my current position. I could no longer deny the fact that i wanted, needed and deserved more. My friend mentioned a company to me for the 3rd time. I had listened to you TED talk and told her I was going to hang up the phone and call that company right now. AND I DID! End result i now have a new job with that company. It is better than any other job I have interviewed for!

I started last week! 5 second rule - ROCKS! Thank you! Juanita

Learning about the #5SecondRule was a turning point for Gabe. After realizing "that I was responsible for everything that happened in my life," Gabe used the Rule to change his life by starting his own Virtual Reality company. Today, he is creating the career of his dreams.

Gabe

Marketing and Branding Consultant | Virtual Reality Developer

Went from a full time marketing manager who was "doing fine," to a connected, dedicated and growing owner of my own Virtual Reality company on my way to fulfilling the career of my dreams.

I was OK with being FINE, I forgot that I was responsible for everything that happened in my life.

Kristin's life has been forever changed because her boyfriend now has a way to battle his drug addiction. Whenever he feels the desire to go "back to one of those drugs," he uses the #5SecondRule to fight his addiction and retrain his mind. He counts backwards 5- 4- 3- 2- 1 to himself to trigger new behavior and "his mindset completely changes and he goes about his day."

Hello,

I saw you at the Scentsy Family Reunion this past summer. My boyfriend and I were in the audience. This story is more about him then me. You have forever changed our lives with the 5-4-3-2-1 rule. He is a recovering drug addict that most people don't know about. Well he finally stopped all the different drugs right before we left for our trip to Nashville, where we saw you. Since that day he uses your 5-4-3-2-1 rule every time he has a desire to go back to one of those drugs. He says it to himself and his mindset completely changes and he goes about his day. Thank you from the bottom of my heart, thank you for sharing your story.

Courage is, in fact, what I needed to get out of bed. It was scary to get out of bed because it meant facing my problems. It was difficult to look myself in the mirror and accept the fact that I was 41 years old and my life and career were in pretty lousy shape. It was overwhelming to consider I might not be able to fix the situation my husband and I were in.

Courage is what my daughter needs to put down the pen in her high school history class and raise her hand. It's what your team needs to escalate its concerns to you and it's what your kids need to tell you what's *really* going on. Putting your online profile up on a dating site or blocking your ex on your phone can feel like an act of bravery. So can adopting new technology for your business or walking in the door of your home and facing your problems head-on instead of pouring a drink and zoning out in front of the TV.

As I began to write this book and started collecting stories of people around the world using the Rule, it became clear that inside every decision there exist five seconds of courage that can change everything in our lives.

The more the word "courage" came up, the more I began to wonder if there was something about one of the most historic moments of courage that would help me better understand the nature of courage itself. The first person that came to mind was Rosa Parks. You probably know the story of how Rosa Parks sparked the modern American Civil Rights Movement on a chilly December evening in 1955 when she quietly refused to give up her seat on the bus for a white passenger.

Her moment of courage teaches us all that it's not the big moves that change everything—it's the smallest ones in your everyday life that do. She didn't plan to do what she did that night. Mrs. Parks described herself as the kind of person who tried to "be as careful as possible to stay out of trouble." The only thing she planned on doing that evening was to get home after a long day at work and have dinner with her husband. It was just an evening, like any other evening—until one decision changed everything.

Curious, I dug in and researched everything I could find about Mrs. Parks, from the National Archives, biographies, radio interviews, and newspaper articles. What I found is incredible. Just weeks after her arrest, she gave a radio interview to Sidney Rogers on Pacifica Radio and the National Archives website has a recording of it. Here's how she described that historic moment in her own words:

As the bus proceeded out of town on the third stop, the white passengers had filled the front of the bus. When I got on the bus, the rear was filled with colored passengers, and they were beginning to stand. The seat I occupied was the first of the seats where the Negro passengers, uh, take as they—on this route. The driver noted that the front of the bus was filled with white passengers, and there would be two or three men standing.

He looked back and…demanded the seats that we were occupying. The other passengers very reluctantly gave up their seats. But I refused to do so…The driver said that if I refused to leave the seat, he would have to call the police. And I told him, "Just call the police."

Then the radio interviewer asked her the million-dollar question:

"What in the world ever made you decide to be the person who after all these years of Jim Crowe and segregation, what made you at that particular moment decide you were going to keep that seat?"

She replied very simply,

"I felt that I was not being treated right and that I had a right to retain the seat that I had taken as a passenger on that bus."

He pressed her again noting that she had been mistreated for years, and wanted to know *what made her decide in that moment*—and in the interview, she paused for a second and then said:

"The time had just come that I had been pushed as far as I stand to be pushed, I suppose."

He asked her if she planned it—and she said,

"No."

He asked her if it just sort of happened. She agreed that it "just sort of happened."

This is a critical detail: *Rosa Parks didn't hesitate or think it through*. It happened so fast, she just listened to her instincts telling her *"I was not being treated right,"* and she pushed herself to follow them.

Since she didn't hesitate, there was no time to talk herself out of it.

Coincidentally, four days later, in that same city of Montgomery, Alabama, on December 5, 1955, there was another five-second decision that changed history.

The Montgomery Improvement Association was formed in response to Mrs. Parks' arrest and a 26-year-old black preacher was voted by his peers to lead the 381-day bus boycott that ensued. On being nominated to lead the boycott that night, the young preacher would later write:

> "It happened so quickly that I did not have time to think it through. It is probable that if I had, I would have declined the nomination."

Thank goodness he didn't think it through. He would become one of the greatest civil rights leaders of all time. His name was Dr. Martin Luther King Jr.

Dr. King was pushed into the spotlight by his peers. Rosa pushed herself. They both experienced the power of a push. It's a moment when your instincts, values, and goals align, and you move so quickly you don't have time or a valid reason to stop yourself.

Your heart speaks and you don't think, you listen to what your heart tells you to do. Greatness is not a personality trait. It's inside all of us and sometimes it's hard for us to see it. Mrs. Parks was described by all who knew her as quiet and shy, and Dr. King famously struggled with self-doubt and fear in the beginning days of the Civil Rights movement.

Reflecting back on the radio that night in 1956, Mrs. Parks said, *"I hadn't thought I would be the person to do this, it hadn't occurred to me."* It probably hasn't occurred to you either what great things you might be capable of achieving at work and in your lifetime. Her example shows us that we are all more than capable of finding the courage to "act out of character" when the moment matters.

It is true, as Rosa Parks explained on air in that 1956 interview, that she was pushed *"as far as I could stand to be pushed"* by a system of discrimination. But in that singular moment, she was pushed forward by something way more powerful: herself.

That's what courage is. It's a push. The kind of push we give ourselves when we stand up, speak up, show up, go first, raise our hand or do whatever feels hard, scary, or uncertain. Do not look at our heroes in history, business, art, and music and assume that somehow they are different than you. It's not true.

Courage is a birthright. It is inside each and every one of us. You were born with it and you can tap into it anytime you want. It's not a matter of confidence, education, status, personality, or profession. It's simply a matter of knowing how to find it when you need it. And when you need it, you'll probably be alone.

It's going to be just you sitting in a meeting at work, standing in your kitchen, riding the subway, looking at your phone, staring at your computer, or thinking about something—and all of sudden, it will happen. Something will go down, and your instincts will come alive. You'll have an urge to act. Your values and your instincts will tell you what you *should* do. And your feelings will scream "NO." That is the push moment. You don't have to have all the answers. You just have to make a decision in the next five seconds.

Dan is alone at his computer thinking about registering for summer classes. He wants to earn his college degree but at the age of 44, the idea of starting as a freshman is nothing short of terrifying.

Courage is what Christine needs as she's sitting in a marketing meeting in Plano, Texas. She has a great idea to share but wonders, *Is this going to sound stupid?*

Tom is standing in a bar in Chicago. The moment he sees her he can't look away. He can either turn back toward his friends and pretend to care about the football game they're discussing, or find the courage to start walking toward her.

The entire sales organization of a financial software company feels discouraged in Nashville. They've hit their numbers three years in a row, and quotas just got raised yet again.

Alice in England needs to push herself out the door to go on a run. She's inspired by her friend on Facebook, but *feels discouraged* by how long it's been since she last exercised.

Halfway around the world, Patel can't stop thinking about a friend whose son just died in a car accident. He doesn't know what to say, and the thought of losing his own son terrifies him. He tells himself, *It will be easier if I wait a few days,* but the urge to pick up the phone, stop by the house…*to do something* lingers.

In China, Sy has just signed on as a distributor for a new skin care line. She has at least a dozen people she wants to call. She looks at her phone and hesitates—*what if they think I'm being pushy?*

In Queensland, Australia, Todd knows exactly what he wants to do with his life, and it isn't studying law, it's physical education. But before Todd can take control of his future, he'll need to face his parents' disappointment.

And Mark is lying in bed in Auckland, Australia, where it's 10:30 p.m. He turns and looks at his wife as she reads her book. He would love to make love to her, but he assumes she's not in the mood; he wants to lean over and kiss her shoulder but he *fears rejection.* He needs courage to lean toward her after so many months of feeling like her roommate.

These stories are real and they are just the tip of the iceberg. They highlight the struggle between our desire to change our lives and our fear of it. They also reveal the power that everyday courage has to transform everything.

Seth Godin once wrote "a different part of our brains is activated when we think about what's possible rather than what's required." I believe the same is true when we think about being courageous, rather than focusing on the fears that stop us. It's the difference between focusing on the solution rather than the problem, and that tiny switch is mentally liberating.

There's something powerful about framing my struggle to get out of bed, Patel's struggle to call his friend, a sales organization's struggle to embrace a higher sales goal, and Alice's struggle to exercise as acts of everyday courage.

After all, courage is just a push.

When you push yourself, you may not change the world, the laws, or spark a civil rights movement but I can guarantee you'll change something equally as important—you'll change yourself.

There is only one YOU.

And there will never be another one.

That's your power.

CHAPTER SIX

WHAT ARE YOU WAITING FOR?

"THE TIME IS ALWAYS RIGHT TO DO WHAT IS RIGHT."

DR. MARTIN LUTHER KING, JR

Tom is celebrating a new piece of business with his colleagues at Stetson's Steakhouse inside the Hyatt Regency Hotel in downtown Chicago. He is crushing his quota for the year and the win today will put the territory he manages ahead on the leaderboard. Four months ago, he threw himself into his job at a financial tech company after his wife moved out. It's been a welcome distraction as he tries to pick up the pieces of his personal life. He turns toward the bartender to order another round, and that's when he sees her.

She's standing just across the bar, laughing with her friends. There's something about her. He can't quite put his finger on it. He thinks about walking over and talking to her, but he hesitates. He starts to wonder if it's too soon to put himself out there. He begins to feel uncertain: *Would a woman that hot go for a guy with two kids?*

Tom has a decision to make and he'll make it in the next five seconds.

In the amount of time it takes to start walking across a bar, Tom could start to rebuild his life. In the amount of time it takes to raise your hand in a meeting, you can change how you are perceived at work. In the amount of time it takes to open your mouth and compliment someone, you could brighten someone's day. And if you don't, the moment will pass, like it did for Blake and now she wants to "kick myself."

Blake
@blakie_g

I thought too much about it and the moment passed and I didn't tell this woman how fabulous she is. She made my day and I didn't thank her.

Blake
@blakie_g

But I didn't say anything. I opened my mouth and no words came out. And I thought about @melrobbins 5 second rule and wanted to kick myself.

Whatever reason you use to hold yourself back—you are wrong. It's not safer to stay quiet. It's not better to keep the peace. It's not futile to try. It's not risky. You are wrong. All your excuses and reasons are wrong. There is no "right time" to improve your life. The moment you move you'll discover your strength. That's the way to bring the REAL you to the table—by pushing the *real* you out of your head and into the world. And the best time to do it, is right now when your heart tells you to move.

We waste so much of our lives waiting for the right time to have the conversation, ask for the raise, bring it up, or start things. It reminds me of that famous Wayne Gretzky quote: *"You miss 100% of the shots you don't take."* Here's the thing—you never regret the shots you do take but you always regret holding back. Anthony realized this the hard way:

 **Anthony**

Tonight I had a chance to give someone my number and I didn't and I will actually forever regret that. WHY IS LIFE SO HARD?! 💔

Life is already hard, yet we make it so much harder when we listen to our fears, we convince ourselves to wait, and we hold our greatest selves back. We all do it. And not just in bars. We hold ourselves back at work, at home, and in our relationships.

The question is, why do we do this? The answer is brutal. You can call it a fear of rejection, or a fear of failure, or a fear of looking bad. The reality is, we hide because we are afraid even to try.

I had a conversation a few months ago with my daughter Kendall that illustrates just how deadly this waiting game can be to your dreams. To give you some background, Kendall is fifteen and a very talented singer. From the moment she wakes up until the moment she goes to bed, she's singing.

Recently, one of her mentors recommended her for an audition with the directors of a musical in New York City. He had placed kids on tour with *Les Misérables, Mary Poppins,* and *Matilda.* He thought Kendall had a very good chance of landing a role.

The second the topic came up, she said she "wanted to audition" but never wrote her mentor back about it. I asked her why she was waiting. It was fascinating and heartbreaking to hear how her thoughts and feelings had trapped her. Funny enough, she wasn't afraid of the audition itself. At least not when she thought about it. It was everything that *might happen* after the audition.

She said that she didn't want to try out because, "What if I didn't make it, Mom? What if I am not as good as I think I am? If I don't audition, at least I can tell myself that I'm amazing—I'm just too lazy to have what I want."

Now we were getting somewhere. The fear of sucking, of not being good enough, of feeling like a loser—none of us wants to face that reality. So we avoid it like the plague. I actually do it with exercise. I can pretend I'm in decent shape as long as I avoid it. The moment I hit the gym I have to face reality. And the reality is that within two minutes of running on a treadmill, I have to go the bathroom and I'm out of breath. I'm not in great shape at all. I have a lot of work to do. That's why we dodge challenges—to protect our egos, even if it means eliminating the possibility of getting what we want.

I listened to Kendall talk about her fear that she wasn't good enough, and then asked her one simple question:

"What If You're Wrong?"

It's a powerful question, and we don't ask it nearly enough. What if you're wrong? What if you audition and you really are as good as everyone says? What if your idea actually is the next million-dollar business? What if you not only meet your quota again this year, but you also actually surpass it? What if being single isn't as scary as you think and your true soulmate is just days away from bumping into you? Are you really going to let your worries stop you from doing the work, having the love life, and being your greatest self? You damn well better not.

And even if you do suck—there's another thing you can say to yourself:

So What!?

So what if you suck? At least you tried. As far as I'm concerned landing the role is irrelevant. Just like the woman Tom saw at the bar is irrelevant. The only thing relevant is *you*. The power is *inside* of you. The only way you access that power is pushing yourself to try. The greatest you shows up at the audition, walks up to the gal or guy at the bar, and raises their hand and their voice at work.

You'll never stop yourself from starting to worry about something. But you can stop yourself from letting those worries drag you into a parade of worries that take control of your mind. You can assert yourself and push yourself to think about something empowering. You step back into the present moment and go for what you want. And you can do it in five seconds flat.

We are all guilty of thinking about getting involved but not doing it. We're all waiting "for the right time." It's total stupidity. In a recent survey, 85% of professional services employees admitted they were withholding critical feedback from their bosses. Why? You already know the answer—they're waiting for the "right time." The same is true for your kids, your spouse, your friends, and your colleagues.

All human beings are wired this way. One of the most insightful and enlightening aspects of Adam Grant's incredible book *Originals: How Non-Conformists Move the World* is when he describes how some our greatest heroes are just like us in this simple regard: they hesitated, doubted themselves, and almost missed the opportunities of their lifetimes because they didn't feel ready. I find it reassuring to know that the people we admire most needed to be pushed through their fears, excuses, and feelings, just like you and me.

You know Michelangelo, the artist who painted the Sistine Chapel in Rome? There's a backstory you might not know. According to Grant, when the Pope asked Michelangelo to paint the Sistine Chapel in 1506, Michelangelo felt so overwhelmed with self-doubt that he not only wanted to wait, but he also actually fled to Florence and hid. The Pope had to stalk Michelangelo and pester him for two years to get him to agree to paint it.

Want to hear another one? How about one related to Apple? In 1977, when an investor offered Steve Jobs and Steve Wozniak funding to launch Apple, Wozniak felt so afraid and uncertain he wanted to "wait a while" before he quit his job. He didn't *feel* ready. He was pushed by "Jobs, multiple friends, and his own parents" to make the leap.

Remember the stories in the last chapter about Dr. Martin Luther King Jr admitting he would have declined the nomination to lead the Montgomery Improvement Association "had he thought it through"? Or Rosa Parks' admission that she never thought "she would be the one to do this"? In the moment, neither one of them stopped to think. They didn't wait to *feel* ready. That's what we all need to do. We are all capable of greatness. I believe that. It is our feelings and fears that convince us now is not the right time and keep us from achieving greatness.

Grant then writes this line in his book, which made my heart feel heavy: "We can only imagine how many Wozniaks, Michelangelos, and Kings never pursued, publicized, or promoted their original ideas because they were not dragged or catapulted into the spotlight." The question to ask yourself is this one:

What Are You Waiting For?

Are you waiting for someone to ask you, drag you, pick you, or catapult you into the spotlight, or are you willing to find the courage to push yourself? Are you waiting to feel ready? Waiting for the right time. Waiting to gain confidence. Waiting to feel like it. Waiting to feel worthy. Waiting until you have more experience.

Sometimes there is no next time, no second chance, or no time out. Stop waiting. It's now or never. When you wait, you aren't procrastinating. You are doing something more dangerous. You are deliberately convincing yourself "now is not the time." You are actively working against your dreams.

Paula could have convinced herself that she would "never qualify" for a great job opportunity. She would have been very wrong.

I just applied for a job I never thought I would qualify for because I figured, "why not just try it?" I didn't focus on my shortcomings but emphasized my qualities and got the job. Previously I would have forgotten about it after 5 seconds and not even tried by the way ;–)

—Paula

By "emphasizing her qualities" instead of focusing on her shortcomings, Paula was able to push past her fears and land the job.

You may think you're protecting yourself from judgment, rejection, or upsetting someone, but when you make excuses and talk yourself into waiting, you are limiting your ability to make your dreams come true. I'm amazed by how much time I've wasted in my life waiting for the right time, waiting until I'm sure, waiting until I think my work is perfect, or waiting until I feel like it.

You may be afraid of finding out that you suck, like my daughter was. Let me tell you what really sucks: being older and regretting that you never went for it. Being 30 and realizing you let fear of what your friends thought keep you from ever really putting yourself out there when you were younger. Friends, by the way, who you never talk to anymore. Being 56 and realizing you should have divorced your spouse ten years ago. Being 45 and wishing you had had the courage to take on a project at work that you now realize would have changed the trajectory of your career. Or sitting in college classes earning a degree to please your parents when knowing in your heart that you want to be doing something else with your life.

There is no right time. There is only right now. You get one life. This is it. And it's not going to begin again. It's up to you to push yourself to make the most of it and the time to do it is right now.

You Validate Your Ideas By Pursuing Them

It's heartbreaking to hear from so many of you with a creative idea or product concept that are waiting for someone else to validate it. It's so sad because waiting for validation will be the death of your dreams. If you have an idea for a show or a book, and you are waiting for an executive at a TV network or a publishing house to pick you, you will lose. It's like Tom in the bar hoping his soulmate will just walk up to him and pick him. Or me waiting until I felt motivated to wake up and get out of bed. Waiting until you are ready will not make it happen. The world doesn't work that way.

The world rewards those who are courageous enough to stop waiting and start. If you dream of being on television, I can tell you from first-hand experience that the TV executive you hope discovers you is actually on YouTube right now looking for someone who didn't wait. The person who has the courage to start, create, and put themselves and their ideas out there is the one who will win.

The only difference between that idea for a novel you want to write and British author E.L. James who wrote the blockbuster *Fifty Shades of Gray* trilogy (that was devoured by nearly every woman on the planet Earth and sold a million copies in four days) is the fact that she didn't wait for permission, the right time, or to feel ready. She didn't wait until she had a book deal. In fact, she started writing erotica on a Twilight-themed blog! She found the courage to start in small ways, and put herself out there over and over until she built the confidence to write a book. And

Fifty Shades of Gray was that book. It was self-published by a working mom who wrote in her free time. Yup.

By the way, that's also how Grammy award-winning musician Ed Sheeran got discovered. He was 15 years old playing songs in a park in England with no permit and no guarantee that anyone would notice. That's how you do it. You push yourself to get out of your comfort zone and you begin. There is no other way. You stop waiting for "the right time" and you start. That's how award-winning *Broad City* landed its hit show on Comedy Central. They acted with courage and started filming 3-minute clips on an iPhone and posting them on YouTube.

And every single YouTube star, from Tyler Oakley, to make-up tutorial phenom Michelle Phan, to "My Drunk Kitchen" host Hannah Hart, to Minecraft narrator "Stampy Cat," will tell you that if they had told themselves to wait until they felt ready or until they had a sponsor, they would still be living a boring life instead creating a life of their dreams and laughing all the way to the bank.

Waiting, thinking, and "almost doing it" don't count. As Kyra explains, to change anything you actually have to do it. #AlmostDoesntCount

---

Kyra

5,4,3,2,1 Go! I almost didn't go to the "block party" my complex held last night because I was exhausted after work... I almost decided not to donate blood at the truck they had there... I almost didn't make the exposure to the nice nurse I met who was also donating, I almost didn't run back to my apartment to get my third party tools to give to her before I left. I almost didn't follow up with her this morning and when she invited me over to go talk to her and her girlfriends about it? I almost didn't go because I was still in my PJ's, had no expert lined up and felt unprepared... But I did and now? I will be entering 2 new PC's tonight and 2 tomorrow and I'm officially NLC qualified for September and am now half way through October! The moral of the story is #almostdoesntcount #justdoit

---

The difference between people who make their dreams come true and those of us who don't is just one thing: the courage to start and the discipline to keep going.

The Rule is a game-changer because it 5- 4- 3- 2- 1 forces you to get out of your head and start and it'll 5- 4- 3- 2- 1 help you keep going.

And that brings us back to Tom at the bar in the Hyatt Regency in Chicago. Will he start walking toward the girl across the room or decide to wait? Well…that depends. It depends on who is making the decision for Tom. Will it be Tom's heart that makes the decision or his head? Will it be Tom's dreams that win or will it be his fears? Rosa Parks offers some amazing advice for moments like this one—Tom needs to do what *"must be done."* Tom knows in his heart what must be done. He needs to start living again.

Waiting won't help. Waiting will only make it worse. When you sit with fear and uncertainty your mind makes it expand; it's called "the spotlight effect" and it's one of the many tricks your brain plays in an attempt to keep you "safe."

The fear Tom feels is real. The uncertainty is scary. The self-doubt can be crippling. No one wants to be rejected or feel like a fool. No one wants to find out that they "suck."

That's why the moment right before you walk into a networking meeting, a party, an interview, a cafeteria, or start walking toward someone you find attractive, it can feel daunting. We think about what could go wrong or how awkward it will feel if no one welcomes us, instead of all the possibilities.

But safety isn't what Tom wants. Tom wants to rebuild his life and find love again and that's going to take courage. As scary as it is taking that first step to the other side of the bar, Tom is about to discover that all the magic, wonder, and joy in life happens the moment he does.

You can feel uncertain and be ready. You can be afraid and do it anyway. You can fear rejection and still go for it.

Five Seconds of Courage Changes Everything

Tom starts counting to himself, "5- 4- 3-…" and by the time he gets to 2, he starts walking across the room. He has no idea what he'll say to her. His heart is racing, but for the first time in a long time he doesn't feel numb, he feels alive. The closer he gets to her, the more his heart races. She turns around just as he reaches her. What happens next is…irrelevant.

It doesn't matter what happens because she either becomes his soulmate or she doesn't. The ending of the story is irrelevant—the *only* thing that matters is the beginning of the story, that Tom made a choice to begin living again. That's how you listen to your heart. Whether you are starting to date again, starting a company, or starting a YouTube channel, you must find the courage to start.

Notice how we desperately want an assurance that Tom "got the girl." It makes for a great movie plot, but "getting the girl" isn't the point. Life isn't a Nicholas Sparks novel. Life is gritty and hard and then suddenly it is brilliant and amazing. Besides, the girl could be engaged. She could be gay. She could be a real bitch. Even if she's amazing and they end up having crazy hot sex or go on to get married, "the girl" is not the source of power in the story. Tom is.

The treasure in your life is buried within *you*. It's not inside of someone else. Tom is the source of power in his life and you are the source of power in yours. You unlock that power when you listen to your instincts and 5- 4- 3- 2- 1 push yourself to honor them. When you discover your "inner true self" it will be the "most important gift of all."

 Melody Fowler I have used the 5 sec rule everyday (multiple times) since Dallas! It has helped me clear out negative thoughts, it has helped me reach out to people and start conversations I might not initiate otherwise, it has brought my inner true self out loud! And that to me has been the most important gift of all, to be me and show my daughter how to do it too!
Thank you Mel!

Jean-Baptiste also saw this. He wrote to me that he realized "that nobody was going to come and get me to live the life that I want to live and that taking action is the only way to create my own space into the world."

Jean-Baptiste

Hello! I just wanted to let you know that i admire the work you do and the ideas you share with world. I'm 19 years old, and watching your ted talk and your other speeches allowed me to realize that nobody was going to come and get me to live the life that i want to live and that taking action is the only way to create my own space into the world. I believe that everybody could bring something new and original to the world we live in. Seriously, you helped. Thank you for that. Keep changing the world one sequin at time.

With love, JB.

Just as Jean-Baptiste said, I also "believe that everybody could bring something new and original to the world we live in." The potential for massive greatness exists inside every single one of us.

The way that you activate the power of you is by finding the courage you need every single day to push yourself forward. When you listen to your instincts (*"get up and face the day, Mel," "suck it up and start walking, Tom," "take care of your nephews, Catherine," "don't give up your seat, Rosa"*)—it's clear what you must do.

There is no debate when you follow what's inside your heart. The only thing that will quiet the chatter in your head is a decision to move. As I said in the very beginning of the book, you really are just one decision away from a completely different life.

We are all so afraid of uncertainty that we want a guarantee before we even try. We want evidence that if we take a risk we will "get the girl" too. Even if Tom gets the girl, it's not proof that you will. "Getting the girl" or "the guy," for that matter, is a numbers game. To play any game, you have to start. To win, you'll need to keep going. If you want to make your dreams come true, get ready for the long game.

Life is not a one-and-done sort of deal. You've got to work for what you want. Do you know the game Angry Birds? Rovio, the brand that created the game, launched 51 unsuccessful games before they developed Angry Birds. How about *The Avengers* star Mark Ruffalo? Do you know how many auditions he did before he landed his *first* role? Almost 600! Even Babe Ruth struck out 1,330 times. My favorite vacuum cleaner is a Dyson. And there's no wonder why it doesn't suck at sucking up the dirt. James Dyson created 5,127 prototypes! What? And this last one will blow your mind. Picasso created nearly 100 masterpieces in his lifetime. But what most people don't know is that he created a total of more than 50,000 works of art.

Did you see the last number? 50,000. That's two pieces of art a day. Success is a numbers game. And you're not going to win it if you keep telling yourself to wait. The more often that you choose courage, the more likely you'll succeed.

When you 5- 4- 3- 2- 1 push yourself forward you'll discover the magic in your life and you open yourself up to the world, to opportunity, and to possibility. You might not get the girl, the part, or the response you wanted but that's not the point. In the end, you'll get something way cooler—you'll discover the power inside of you.

Hold on. Let me over think about it.

CHAPTER SEVEN

YOU'LL NEVER FEEL LIKE IT

"IT TAKES COURAGE TO GROW UP AND BECOME

WHO YOU REALLY ARE."

E.E. CUMMINGS

It's a hot afternoon in Plano, Texas, and a woman named Christine is sitting in a meeting at work. Her boss has called the meeting to discuss ideas to help close a massive piece of consulting business. It's down to two companies and the decision will be made next week. Christine is listening and taking notes when suddenly she thinks of an out-of-the-box idea:

What if we create a custom Snapchat geo-filter and tag it to the prospect's office building…everyone at the building using Snapchat will see it and that will create buzz about our company.

Her mind starts to race with all kinds of cool things that they could do. The conversation among her colleagues is winding down and the VP of Business Development says, "These are great suggestions, anyone else?"

Christine has a decision to make and she'll make it in the next five seconds

She knows she should jump into the conversation, but first she stops to think. *Is this going to sound crazy? No one else suggested anything even close to this kind of thing.* She shifts in her chair. *Is there a reason no one else has mentioned Snapchat?* Now she's questioning whether she should share the idea at all.

In the next five seconds, Christine will either decide to say nothing, a pattern that's become a habit at work, or she will find the courage to speak up. Plus, Christine has a goal. She wants to advance in her career and is worried that she's going to get "passed over" for more senior roles if she doesn't improve her executive presence. She's been spending a lot of time figuring out what she needs to do and she wrote to me because she was struggling with her ability to make herself do it. Her confidence is taking a nosedive.

She had devoured fantastic books like *Lean In, Tribes, Daring Greatly,* and *The Confidence Code.* She has attended women's conferences, listened intently to her mentor, and practiced power posing in her mirror at home. Thanks to all this research and reading, Christine *knows what she needs to do* (share strategic ideas, be proactive, lean in, be more visible, and volunteer for projects that stretch her), and she knows why she needs to do these things.

You're probably wondering why on earth Christine didn't just speak up when she had the chance. Great question.

The answer is simple: she's losing the battle with her feelings. Christine isn't struggling with speaking. She's struggling with self-doubt. Of course Christine knows how to speak in a meeting. What she doesn't know how to do is beat the feelings that are stopping her.

If you've ever wondered why it's so hard to make yourself do the things that you know will solve your problems and improve your life, the answer is simple. It's your feelings. None of us realize it, but we make almost every single decision not with logic, not with our hearts, not based on our goals or dreams—but with our feelings.

And our feelings in the moment are almost never aligned with what's best for us. Take Christine as an example. She knows what's best for her: to speak up. In the moment, however, her feelings are making her second-guess herself. Study after study shows that we opt for what feels good now or feels easier rather than doing the things that we know in our hearts will make us better in the long run.

The moment that you realize your feelings are the problem, you now have the ability to beat them. Look at how quickly Christine's feelings rose in that meeting in Plano, Texas. In less than five seconds, self-doubt started to fill her mind. It happens to all of us. And once you understand the role feelings play in how you make a decision, you will be able to beat them. Here's what you need to know:

You Make Decisions Based On How You Feel

We like to think that we use logic or consider our goals when we make decisions but that's not the case. According to neuroscientist Antonio Damasio, it's our feelings that decide for us 95% of the time. You feel before you think. You feel before you act. As Damasio puts it, human beings are "feeling machines that think" not "thinking machines that feel." And that's how you ultimately make decisions— based on *how you feel.*

Damasio studied people who had damage to their brains and couldn't feel any emotions at all and he discovered something fascinating—none of his research subjects could make a decision. They could describe logically what they *should do* and the *pros and cons of the choice*, but they couldn't actually make a choice. The simplest decisions like *"what do I want to eat?"* were paralyzing.

What Damasio discovered is paramount for you to understand. Every time we have a decision to make, we subconsciously tally all the pros and cons of our choices and then make a gut call, *based on how we feel*. This happens in a nanosecond. That's why none of us catches it.

For example, when you ask yourself the question, *"What do I want to eat?"* you are actually asking yourself, *"What do I feel like eating?"* Similarly, I wasn't asking, *"Should I get up?"* Subconsciously, I was asking, *"Do I feel like getting up?"* Tom wasn't asking, *"Do I want to walk over to her?"* Subconsciously he was asking, *"Do I feel like walking over to her?"* Christine was doing the same thing at work. She wasn't asking, *"Should I share my idea?"* Subconsciously, she was asking, *"Do I feel like sharing my idea?"*

Huge difference. And that explains why change is hard. Logically, we know what we *should* do, but *our feelings about doing it* make our decision for us. Your feelings will make the decision before you even realize what happened. How you feel in the moment is almost never aligned with your goals and your dreams. If you only act when you feel like it, you will never get what you want.

You must learn how to separate what you feel from the actions that you take. The #5SecondRule is a remarkable tool in this regard.

The moment you *feel too tired*, you'll decide not to go for a run, **but 5- 4- 3- 2- 1- GO, and you could make yourself go for one.**

If you *don't feel like* attacking the to-do list on your desk, you won't, **but 5- 4- 3- 2- 1-GO, and you can force yourself to start working on it.**

If you *don't feel worthy*, you'll decide not to tell him what you really think, **but 5- 4- 3- 2- 1-GO, and you can make yourself say it.**

If you don't learn how to untangle your feelings from your actions, you'll never unlock your true potential.

Here's how feelings keep you from changing. When you stop to consider *how you feel*, you stop moving toward your goal. Once you hesitate, you'll start thinking about what you need to do, you'll weigh the pros and cons, you'll consider *how you feel about what you need to do*, and you'll talk yourself out of doing it.

I have said it before, and I'll say it again because it is so important. You aren't battling your ability to stick to a diet, execute a business plan, repair a broken marriage and rebuild your life, hit your sales goals, or win over a bad manager—you are battling your feelings about doing it. You are more than capable of doing the work to change anything for the better, despite how you feel.

You can't control how you feel. But you can always choose how you act.

Ever wonder how pro athletes achieve so much? Part of it is talent and practice, but another key element is a skill that you and I need in our lives—the ability to separate from our emotions and push our bodies and mouths to move. They may feel tired as the football game drags into the fourth quarter, but they don't act tired. Feelings are merely suggestions, ones the greatest athletes and teams ignore. To change, you must do the same. You must ignore how you feel, and as Nike would tell you, *Just Do It* anyway.

Everyone struggles with their feelings of self-doubt. Just ask Lin-Manuel Miranda, creator of the smash hit *Hamilton* that won 11 Tony Awards in 2016. It took him six years to write *Hamilton*. You may dream of writing the next *Hamilton*, and you very well might. Just don't forget that it took Miranda six years to write that show. And he had to battle his feelings of self-doubt every step of the way.

He recently put up this post on his Twitter page. It's a post of a conversation between Miranda and his wife, Vanessa. Three years before *Hamilton* debuted to sell-out crowds and $1,000 tickets, Miranda was still writing the musical and he was struggling with his feelings of self-doubt:

"I have a hard time finding the balance between not beating myself up when it doesn't happen as fast as I'd like it to, and not wasting time while I wait for it to happen."

What did Miranda do? He pushed himself and kept writing. That's why he posted this on his page: to remind everyone that we are all the same. We all struggle with the same self-defeating feelings and the only way out is through. So, 5- 4- 3- 2- 1 suck it up and *"Get back to your piano."*

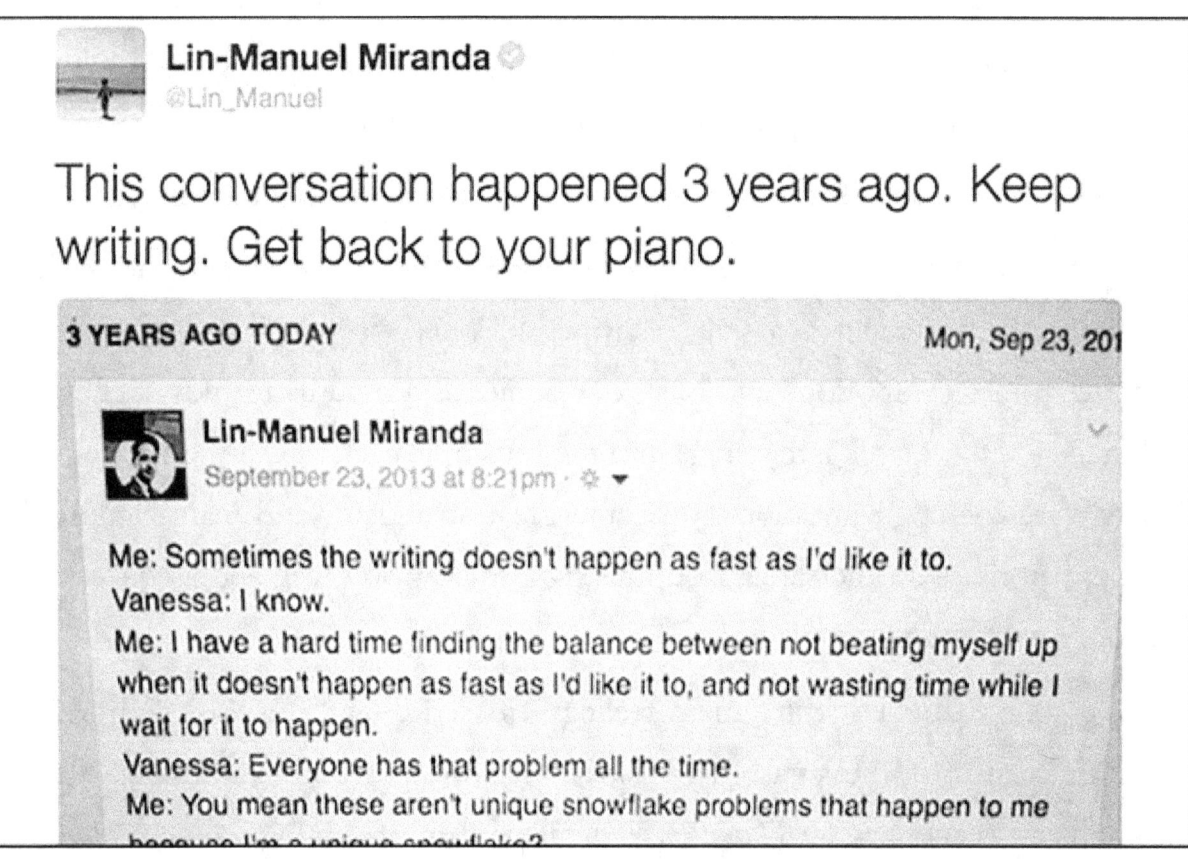

I love what his wife said too: "Everyone has that problem all the time." She's right. We all doubt ourselves. That is the truth. The biggest mistake you could make is to buy into the lies your feelings are telling you. Do not wait until you feel like it. 5- 4- 3- 2- 1 *Get back to your piano.*

Let's go back to that meeting in Plano, Texas, where Christine has a decision to make. In the past, as soon as she felt uncertain, she would have just looked down at her notepad, said nothing, and in five seconds, the moment would have been over. If one of her colleagues had raised a similar idea (as colleagues often do), she'd spend the afternoon beating herself up for not talking.

But today, Christine does something different. She dreads what she is about to do and she can feel the five second window closing as her own brain fights her. Her stomach is in knots as she applies the Rule.

She starts counting backwards silently in her head to quiet the self-doubt and to switch the gears in her brain.

5..4..3..2..1..

The counting interrupts her normal pattern of behavior, distracts her from her fears, and creates a moment of deliberate action. By asserting control in that moment, she activates her prefrontal cortex so that she can drive her thoughts and actions. Then she opens her mouth and says, *"I have an idea."*

Everyone turns and looks at her, and Christine feels like she might just die right there. She forces herself to keep moving forward. She sits up a little taller, takes up a little more space by sliding her elbows wider across the table (as power posing suggests we do), and starts to speak: *So I had this idea, you know how statistically all these Millennials are using Snapchat as a platform to …*

Everyone listened to her idea, asked a few questions, and then her boss said, *"Thanks, Christine. Very interesting suggestion. Anyone else?"* On the outside, nothing earth-shattering happened, but on the inside something life-changing did. She discovered the courage she needed to become the person she always wanted to be at work—a rock star.

What Christine said isn't the point. It's that she said anything at all that makes this moment powerful. Sharing her idea for a social media campaign changed something way more important than the marketing strategy of a company. It changed Christine. It not only changed how she behaved, but it also changed how she viewed herself. It even changed her mindset. This is how you build confidence —one five-second move at a time.

She used the Rule to reach deep inside of herself to find a little courage. And by speaking up, when normally she'd hold back, she proved to herself on a random afternoon in a conference room in Plano, Texas, that she was in fact good enough and smart enough to contribute ideas at work.

It was a small but monumental step. And it took courage. The Rule is HOW she took a risk and was able to apply the advice that we all know works. It was HOW she leaned in as Sheryl Sandberg urges, outsmarted the lizard brain as Seth Godin implores, acted like an "Original" as Grant champions, and dared greatly as Brené Brown empowers us to do.

I said early on that the Rule is a tool that creates immediate behavior change. And that's exactly how Christine used it. That's how you'll use it too. By being deliberate, Christine was able to beat the feelings that normally stopped her and become more assertive in her career. The more that she uses the Rule to express her ideas, the more confident that she will become.

Confidence is a skill that you build through action. Social psychologist Timothy Wilson writes about a psychological intervention, *"do good, be good"* that dates to Aristotle. Its premise is based on changing people's behavior first, which in turn changes their self-perception of the kind of person that they are based on the kinds of things that they do.

This is precisely why the #5SecondRule is your ally. It is a tool for action and for behavior change aligned with your goals and commitments. It is not a tool for thinking, and at the end of the day, you are going to need to do more than think if you want to change your life.

Wilson clearly agrees. He has said that, "our minds aren't stupid. It's not like you can just tell your mind, 'Think Positively.' You've got to nudge it a little more along." I believe you must do more than nudge. You must push right through the feelings that stop you and do the work to break the habits that hold you back. And then, you need to replace each and every one of these destructive habits with a habit of courage.

At the next meeting, Christine will need to practice everyday courage. She will have something to say and she'll feel uncertain and uncomfortable. She will doubt herself as she is about to share her ideas, and then, she'll hesitate and feel herself resist. That's the push moment. It's a moment when your values and goals will align, but your feelings will tell you "NO!" Christine will need to use the #5SecondRule to push herself to speak.

The more that she uses the Rule, the faster she will break her habit of staying silent in meetings and replace it with a new habit: courage. The more that Christine is able to express her true self and bring out the ideas inside her, the more alive, connected, and empowered she'll become.

Nate knows exactly how empowering that feels—he is using the #5SecondRule "everyday now" to push himself to grow his wellness business:

 Omg yes...I used this thing everyday now. I just used it today to meet a sharp looking cold market prospect at the hosptial I work at. She was a patient waiting to be waited on and I approached her, sparked up a convo, and got her contact information to keep in touch and eventually share business material with at a later date.

Pushing herself to "get out of my comfort zone" is how Carol found the courage to achieve one of her #lifegoals #bucketlist—presenting to her nursing colleagues at a professional conference.

When Alexandra was invited to give a presentation at work, her head was full of excuses. In "a matter of 5,4,3,2,1" she acted on a "moment that changed everything"—and that gave her the confidence to teach "a post graduation class!"

When I was invited to give my first presentation (about online marketing) I thought: "Oh cool, but will I really do this? It's not 100% my topic... and it is in another town... and I will have to wake up EARLY on a SATURDAY! And plus, I already have a super busy and tiring week ahead of me, when will I work on my Keynote presentation? And just one more tiny detail: are they gonna like it? Maybe laugh at me?"

Then in a matter of 5,4,3,2,1, I stood up and thought to myself: "Mel Robbins would have said YES without even blinking!" And that's what I did! It was all about that one moment that changed everything! With the help of my amazing husband I set up the presentation, looked it over a thousand times, took my time, practiced in front of the mirror and I am so proud to say that the lecture on Online Marketing Investments was a success! After that I got invited to more and more presentations and even taught a post graduation class with the school!

Thanks for all the videos, book and social media posts Mel, really changed my NOs to YESses!!

Here's a picture of that first presentation! Keep me posted!

XO Alex

The reason why it is so freeing to use the #5SecondRule is because you are not only seizing the moment, you are also taking ownership of your life. You are changing your "NOs to YESes." As Jim says, "never underestimate the power of you"—he's used the Rule to beat "analysis paralysis" and have "one incredible year."

 Jim Goldfuss Mel Robbins 5-second rule has made for one incredible year for me. The things I have done and gotten involved in, while they require activity and commitment on my part, using it to prevent analysis paralysis and second guessing is huge. Never underestimate the power of you, and always use the tools successful people use to accomplish your goals! So pumped with how this year is going!!!!!!

As Wilson and Aristotle said, "Do good, be good." Change your behavior first because when you do, you change how you perceive yourself. That's exactly what Anna Kate discovered while using the #5SecondRule. She's a marketing professional who used to stay quiet when the room was watching, worried that her colleagues would think she's "silly and inexperienced" only to learn that once she found the courage to change her behavior at work, something she never expected happened—her "creativity flourished."

"Hi Mel,

Here is my 5 Second rule story:

While I reluctantly drag myself out of bed (in 5 seconds) in order to do my 30 before 7:30 (inspired by you!) and other morning routines, my career has been impacted the most by the 5 second rule.

I'm in marketing, so we are constantly on alert for new ideas. Each new idea can take off and develop into a full on campaign garnering major results for our clients. Yep, just one little inkling. In order to keep it all together, I like to carry a small notebook in my bag with me wherever I go and use it to jot down quick tasks but mostly ideas.

With the 5 Second Rule, I don't think it out or consider the long term life of my idea, nor do I send it up the ladder for approval - I'll deal with that later. I just need to get it on paper. Later, I revisit and take the time to evaluate a sound strategy.

I used to be such a sissy when it came to sharing ideas or even writing them down! I was self-conscious and worried about what people would think, or if they would see me as silly and inexperienced. Since I have casted my scaredy cat syndrome aside, my creativity has flourished. Now, I can't remember what I was so worried about in the first place.

Thank you for the 5 Second Rule!

P.S. My team actually digs my ideas :)

Anna Kate"

You can feel like a "scaredy cat," but 5- 4- 3- 2- 1 act brave. At the heart of everyday courage is a choice. Five seconds at a time you make a decision to do, say, or pursue what's truly important to you. That's why there's such a tight bond between courage and confidence. Every time you face doubt and 5- 4- 3- 2- 1 right past it, you prove to yourself that you are capable. Every time that you beat fear and 5- 4- 3- 2- 1 do it anyway, you display inner strength. Every time you smash your excuses and 5- 4- 3- 2- 1 say it, you honor the greatness inside of you that wants to be heard. That's how confidence grows—one small, courageous move at a time.

~~Should have Could have Would have~~ Did.

CHAPTER EIGHT

HOW TO START USING THE RULE

"WHETHER YOU THINK YOU CAN OR YOU

CAN'T, YOU'RE RIGHT."

HENRY FORD

The fastest way to implement the #5SecondRule is to start by using it the exact same way I did. Here's a simple Wake Up Challenge that you can do tomorrow morning to jumpstart your use of the Rule. Just set your alarm 30 minutes earlier than usual, and the moment it rings count 5- 4- 3- 2- 1 push yourself out of bed.

Change Is Simple, Not Easy

There are a few reasons why this challenge is important.

First, there's no wiggle room. The challenge is straightforward. It's just you, the alarm clock, and 5- 4- 3- 2- 1. If you fail, it's because you made a decision to blow off the #5SecondRule.

Second, if you can change your morning routine, you can change anything. Change requires you to act deliberately, despite how you feel. If you can master that in one area of your life, you can do it in any area that you are trying to improve.

Third, I want you to experience a concept called "activation energy" and feel how hard it really is to push yourself to do simple things. In chemistry, "activation energy" is the minimum amount of energy required to begin a chemical reaction. Chemists have found that this initial amount of energy is much higher than the average amount of energy needed to keep the reaction going. What does that have to do with getting up? A lot. The initial amount of energy to push yourself out of bed is much higher than the energy you exert once you're up and moving.

Legendary psychologist Mihaly Csikszentmihalyi applied this concept to human behavior, blaming activation energy as one of the reasons why making change is so hard. He defines activation energy as that "initial huge push of energy that's required to change"—whether it's to get a stalled car to move forward or yourself out of a warm bed in the morning.

Jerome from the Philippines wrote:

"It feels uncomfortable because my body and my mind are not ready for this kind of rule. But I'm willing to practice it."

That first bout of activation energy is so uncomfortable, but I want you to feel that resistance so you learn what it's like to push yourself.

If you don't get that huge push (like you did as a kid when your mother turned off the TV and said, "It's a beautiful day, get outside and go do something.") your brain will inevitably take you down the path of doing nothing.

When you start to count 5- 4- 3- 2- 1, it is the beginning of a chain reaction that not only awakens the prefrontal cortex, but also gets you ready to make that physical "initial huge push" that's required to change.

When you get up the moment that alarm rings, it gives you personal power. This one small act of getting up when the alarm rings demonstrates that you have the inner strength to do what needs to be done. Plus, as Emma discovered, it will give you a "much more positive outlook on the day."

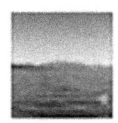 **Emma**

Hi Mel, I listened to your Ted talk last night, and woke this morning for the first time in.. Years.. To my alarm without hitting the snooze button. I've never had a more positive outlook on the day! I'm excited to try this approach for all aspects of my life!
I just wanted to share with you that your words and lessons in living are reaching people all over the world!

That's also what Tracey experienced. By waking up at 5 a.m. and using the Rule to push her out of bed and to the gym, Tracy was able to start her day on a positive note.

 **tracy**

Started the day with an early morning workout…and a little help from the #5SecondRule thank you, @melrobbins!!

If you can't get yourself out of bed, then you'll never be able to pursue all of the other changes that you want to make in your life. And if you take that simple step of taking control of your mornings, you'll catalyze a chain of events that leads to change everywhere.

How To Set Yourself Up for Success

1. Before you go to bed, place your alarm clock in another room and set it for 30 minutes earlier than you normally wake up. Even though it isn't easy to "drag your ass out of bed," as Patty describes, you must push yourself to complete the challenge.

 **Patty**

Just listened to you on TED-I'll be cursing you when I wake up 30 minutes earlier tomorrow, but I'll drag this "fine" ass out of bed!

You might be wondering why I want you to start this exercise by setting your alarm 30 minutes earlier. The reason is simple. I want it to *feel* hard, as if you literally have to drag yourself out of bed, just like Patty said.

2. Tomorrow morning, as soon as the alarm sounds, open your eyes and start counting backwards…5- 4- 3- 2- 1. Throw off the covers, get up, and walk out of your bedroom. Start your day. No delay. No pillow over the head. No lingering, no snooze, no crawling back into bed.

Here's what you can expect. As soon as that alarm goes off, you'll think about how you *feel* about getting up. You'll think, *"this Wake Up Challenge is stupid."* You'll *feel tired.* You'll try to convince yourself to *"start tomorrow."*

Just like Tim, you will "not want to get up"—but the #5SecondRule will help you win the battle with your feelings by giving you something to do that helps you get out of bed.

>  Good morning! I wanted to let you know that I used the 5 second rule this morning. My alarm went off at 4:30 am to head to the gym. I did not want to get up, then the 5 second rule popped in my head and I immediately got up. Just wanted to say thanks for that!

Once the #5SecondRule popped into his head, Tim was able to immediately get up and head to the gym. A lot of us have a "just don't feel like it" attitude in life. In those moments, the Rule will help you take action like it does for Jessica:

"I have found that the 5-4-3-2-1-GO helps on those days when an "I just don't feel like it" attitude creeps in which is everyday, so again, THANK YOU!"

That "I just don't feel like it" attitude has a way of taking over your entire day and that's another reason why this use the Rule is so important. It has a trickledown effect on the rest of your life. Just ask Stephen, who wrote to me about the night before he first tried the Wake Up Challenge.

> I watched your Tedx speech on youtube. Truly inspiring. I'll be waking up at 6:30 tomorrow morning and tossing the covers off. No snooze.
>
> - Stephen

I asked him how waking up early went. He said "it sucked" when he first tried it but over time, it has "made a huge difference." His "mindset literally changed in the span of a few minutes" and since starting the Wake Up Challenge, he has found a new job that has allowed him to "start living life."

How did it go? It sucked. I hate mornings. I've also hated nearly every job I've ever had. I always settle and rarely pursue my passions. I've always been "fine".

I was out of work for 4 months when I sent you the message about getting out of bed at 6:30. I won't say I haven't slept in since then, but it's made a huge difference. I had a mindset that I wouldn't be able to get a new job that I cared about that would pay enough for us to cover our bills, save for retirement and live life. That first morning was terrible, but only for the first few minutes. My mindset literally changed in the span of a few minutes. I was up, ready to conquer the world. Since then, I'm in a new position working for a company and selling a service that I strongly believe in. And the income potential not only pays the bills, but we'll also be able to save for retirement and start living life and having fun again.

I guess if I were to sum it all up for you, it would be this. I love helping others and I've long had visions of doing that through business by gaining and sharing knowledge, wealth and resources with others to allow them to pursue their passions. As of September 12th the snooze button has been broken and autopilot no longer exists. Watch out world, here I come and I'm bringing friends.

As you just read, for Stephen, "the snooze button has been broken and autopilot no longer exists"—and that has made all the difference. Stephen isn't just waking up earlier. He's changed from a guy who used to "always settle and rarely pursue my passions" to a person who has taken his life into his own hands, one five-second decision at a time. And it all started with getting up right when the alarm rang.

If you can get up on time, start your day powerfully, plan ahead, think about your goals, and focus on yourself, all before you get bogged down in your daily routine, then you will simply accomplish more. This is the first step to taking control of your life.

Remember, while I created the Rule to help me get out of bed, the #5SecondRule is about something far greater than waking up on time. It's about waking up the power of you and using it to shake up your life.

After you try the Wake Up Challenge, let me know what you discover about yourself using #5SecondRule. You might find, like Stephen did, that it "sucked," but over time, I guarantee this one small change will make "a huge difference."

Now that you know how to get started, on a basic level, the next three parts of the book will dive deeper into how you can use the Rule to achieve specific goals including increasing productivity, beating the fear, feeling happier, and enriching your relationships.

~~I'm tired.~~
~~It's too cold.~~
~~It's too hot.~~
~~It's raining.~~
~~It's too late.~~
Let's go.

PART3
COURAGE CHANGES YOUR BEHAVIOR

HOW TO BECOME THE MOST PRODUCTIVE PERSON YOU KNOW

I like to say that the #5SecondRule is "change agnostic." It will work with any kind of behavior change that you are trying to make happen. The applications of the #5SecondRule are only limited by your imagination. If you want to adopt a positive new habit, just use the Rule to 5- 4- 3- 2- 1 and push yourself to do it.

You can also use the Rule to pull yourself away from destructive behavior like gambling, drinking, drugs, and impulsive behavior like micromanaging your team, snapping in frustration, and binge watching too many TV shows. Just 5- 4- 3- 2- 1 to assert control and shift your focus away from the destructive or impulsive behavior. Then turn and walk away from it. Like all change, it's simple—not easy, and the Rule will help you get it done.

There are three behavior changes that we receive emails about constantly: health, productivity, and procrastination. I address them in this section of the book. You'll learn the step-by-step approach to how you can use the #5SecondRule in combination with some recent research-based strategies to improve these three major areas of your life.

First, you'll learn the secret to improving your health. You're not going to like it, but it works—and you'll see posts of people all around the globe who are using the #5SecondRule to do some pretty remarkable things for themselves.

Second, you'll learn how to increase your productivity using the #5SecondRule, and the latest research on focus, productivity, and your brain. There's a particular fact in there about the snooze button and how it impacts your productivity that will really surprise you.

Third, you'll dive into a subject that plagues us all—procrastination. You'll learn about the two forms of procrastination, and the step-by-step method for how you can use the #5SecondRule in combination with 19 years of research to beat procrastination once and for all.

Everything you are about to learn can be implemented immediately and is backed by science. To reach your potential, you'll have to push yourself—there is no other way.

Either you run the day or the day runs you.

CHAPTER NINE

IMPROVE YOUR HEALTH

"COURAGE IS THE COMMITMENT TO BEGIN WITHOUT ANY GUARANTEE OF SUCCESS."

JOHANN WOLFGANG VON GOETHE

Almost half of the messages I have received are from people, just like you and me, who want to improve their health. Whether it's to slim down, pump up, drop weight, lower cholesterol, heal yourself from illness, eat healthier, or improve strength and flexibility—whatever it is, you can use the #5SecondRule to get it done.

The fact is that thinking about being healthier won't make you healthier. Even meditation, which is a mental exercise, still requires that you DO IT. There is no getting around this. You must take action.

The irony is that in no other area of our lives is there more information, support, research, options, or free content than on the subject of health and wellness. You could Google "diet," download the top 20 search results, print them out, put them on a dart board, and follow whatever diet the dart hits. The diet, if you actually follow it, will work. The problem is never the diet. The problem is always your *feelings* about dieting. The same is true about exercising.

Just like Ana, we "never feel like working out" and we let these feelings get in the way of our desires to become healthier. Using the #5SecondRule, Ana pushed herself to 5- 4- 3- 2- 1 and got back on the bike:

almuzel
Kor180 >

♥ 36 likes

almuzel I never "feel" like working out. But today I had the pleasure of hearing @melrobbinslive speak at the @visitaustintx luncheon - Her "5 Second Rule" is inspiring. "Everyone knows what they need to do in order to achieve change but 'feelings' get in the way". So, 5..4..3..2..1, I'm back on the bike. Apologies for the person next to me having to listen to my hyperventilating - it's been a minuet 🚴 📷 @kor180 .

Yes, you may hyperventilate as you pedal, but who cares? It sounds better than making excuses at home.

Every single diet, exercise program, gym circuit, workout class, physical therapy regimen, cross-training routine, meditation program, and yoga flow will improve your health. But here's the catch—YOU HAVE TO DO IT. And believe me, I get it. I loathe exercise, especially if it's cold or raining outside. I hate it as much as I hate getting out of bed. Without the #5SecondRule, I'd never do it.

Why is getting healthy so hard? You already know the answer—your feelings. If you *feel deprived* of bread, you won't stick to your gluten-free diet. The second you consider *how you feel* about eating salad for the next 113 days, you'll convince yourself not to do it. The moment you scan today's CrossFit workout and consider *how you feel* about doing three sets of 45 burpees with a bunch of people in a parking lot—you won't feel like walking out the door and going.

Will sticking to a diet make you happy? Absolutely. Will seeing your friends at CrossFit and working out make you happy? You better believe it will. Just ask Melanie, who had trouble getting "off the damn couch" before finding the Rule.

> Dear Mel,
>
> I just wanted to say thank you. Thank you for saying it in a language I can relate. For making me get off the damn couch and out of my head. For experiencing momentum and just be my awesome self! Relief. Freedom and breakthroughs!

And once she did get moving, Melanie experienced "Freedom and breakthroughs," something that we all want. The moment you accept the fact that we just want to do the things that *feel easy*, you realize the secret to getting healthy is simple—you'll never feel like it, you just have to 5- 4- 3- 2- 1-GO!

Blowing off the gym, hitting the In-n-Out Burger drive-thru, and wasting time on Facebook is a hell of lot easier than hyperventilating in a spin class or cutting out sugar from your diet. If you want to lose weight, follow a diet, and regularly exercise, there's only one thing you must do: Stop thinking about how you feel. Your feelings don't matter. The only thing that matters is what you DO.

Erika realized this. Even after starting her weight loss journey, she found herself "losing all motivation to get my workouts in" and "always had an excuse" why she couldn't hit the gym.

Hi Mel!

I'm such a huge fan of yours, I saw you on CNN last year and was intrigued. I've been following you on twitter for about a year now and your inspirational tweets help so much but what has really helped is your #5secondrule.

I finally got my butt into gear this year and started to lose weight that I had tacked on over the last couple of years. I've lost 30 pounds this year and despite that, I found myself losing all motivation to get my work outs in. I always had an excuse- I worked too late, I didn't have enough time, blah..blah..blah.

I watched your video about weight loss on your blog a few weeks ago and you were spot on about every damn thing. I'm never going to feel like working out but if I want to see continued results, I need to get those workouts in.

I've been using your #5secondrule and today marks day 7 of not missing a workout. Some days I still don't want to workout but I have goals and if I convince myself to get that workout in within the first 5 seconds, it gets done.

Can't wait for your book!

Best,
Erika

Once she realized that she was "never going to feel like working out," Erika was able to find 5 second windows of opportunity and then push herself to act on them. Exercise is 100% mental. Your body won't go where your mind doesn't push it. That's why the #5SecondRule is game changing for your health.

Here's HOW you use it…

5- 4- 3- 2- 1-GO and get to the gym.

5- 4- 3- 2- 1-GO and put down the donut and eat a grilled chicken breast.

5- 4- 3- 2- 1-GO and walk away from the bakery even though the bread and desserts are seducing you like a siren.

There are people all over the world who are fatter, lazier, and more out of shape than you who used 5- 4- 3- 2- 1 to change themselves into a totally different body, mindset, and life.

Like Charlie. This guy first reached out to me weighing 383 pounds. His waist was 54 inches. Look at the photos in the following Facebook post and you'll see how heavy he was.

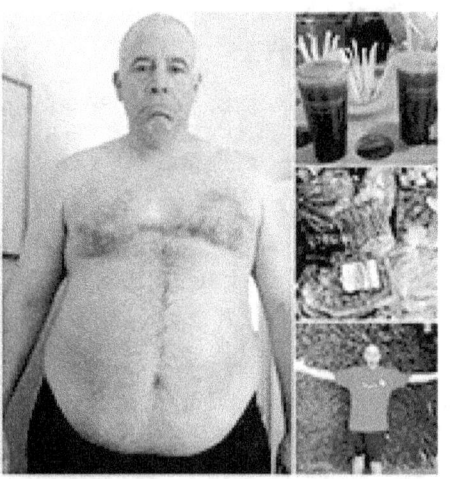

Imagine how horrible he felt. Now look at the other photo of him in the bottom photo—celebrating his life. He is literally a different human being. How'd he do it? By drinking drinks that taste like grass. Yuck, you might say. But that's what it took for him to reach his goal. Today he runs a business called Juicing Strong that helps people become their healthiest selves.

For 529 straight days, this guy pushed himself to keep the promise he made to himself. Why? Not because he felt like it—but because he said he would. Imagine if

Charlie spent the last 529 days *thinking* about losing 176 pounds instead of juicing. What would have happened? Nothing. Alexandra also found her way to a healthier lifestyle by juicing:

Hello There! Alexandra from Brazil!

About my 5 second rule experience:

Every single day I have to spend at least one hour juicing! yes, green, purple, orange, red fresh juices changed my life, and I love them, but life is busy.

So everyday around 5:30pm I am looking at a full email box with marketing plans and reports to send out and aaaalmost go like "maybe i'll just skip the juice today.." BUT NO! NO WAY!
I breathe and think: the emails aren't going anywhere, and nobodys gonna get injured if i delay the report for 2 hours.. so its all about 5, 4, 3, 2, GO JUICING. And it works.. every single day :)

Charlie and Alexandra both found that when you follow your instincts to lead a healthier lifestyle by taking a courageous action, change starts to happen in your life.

It takes courage to start something, it takes courage to stick with it, and it definitely takes courage to share it with the world. That's what Pakinam described to me. Courage is what it required to lose weight because sometimes, as Pakinam writes, the gap between where you are and where you want to be can seem so huge, that we can't even face how much work we have to do:

Hi Mel,

For my entire life I have been over weight. Now I am trying to diet for the first time in my life. I feel lost and trapped, but I keep on going. I have a massive feeling of insecurity and vulnerability. Can you please explain this?

The short answer is that the gap between the person you are now and the person you want to become can seem so big that it feels impossible to bridge that gap. Feeling this way is normal, but allowing those feelings to take over your mind is a form of self-abuse.

That's why I love Charlie and that photo of his bare belly hanging over his shorts. Anyone can bridge the gap between the numbers on the scale with a push. Let Charlie's example inspire you to start today. And let his results encourage you to stick with it.

I have someone else I want you to meet. Mark is using his Instagram friends to hold himself accountable. Five thousand pushups in a month? Holy cow! I can barely do five a day, #exercisegoals.

fujfocus Deciding to take my fitness to another level by announcing to my Facebook nation that I would do 5000 push-ups, 2000 pull-ups and run 200 kilometers in the month of July. All of this while vacationing with my kids half the month and trying to finish my book on increasing business value and selling a business which by the way started because of your 5 second rule which is so powerful. Can't wait to read your book @melrobbinslive . I'm living proof that your brilliant advice works. Love you Mel!!

The discipline of daily exercise will also help his other personal and professional goal of "trying to finish my book on increasing business value and selling." Every day that Mark exercises, he'll have a brain that's primed to help him finish writing that book. Go Mark! Keep us posted when your book is available.

Maybe 5,000 push-ups in one month is a little overwhelming because it might literally kill you. No problem. How about just taking on a fitness challenge? Check out Anouk—she's on week three of hers. She is telling us the simple truth about health and exercise: "I really really really didn't feel like it but did it anyway BOOM BOOM BOOM."

BOOM to you Anouk, you rock girl. And you rock too—when you push yourself to take action when you don't feel like it.

If you feel overwhelmed by the thought of taking this on for real, meet Alice. She's "a 19-year-old girl from the UK" who wrote to me because she had been in a "really bad place." Here's how she described it:

> *I suffer with anxiety and agoraphobia and they really took their toll on me. I gained about 30lbs, which made me even more miserable and I stayed indoors even more. Additionally, I felt pressured by my parents to do a certain degree at a certain university and convinced myself I was fine doing this in order to please them…I watched your video and it really made me think, is this really what I want? Am I really 'fine' being the size I am? Do I deserve to get what I want?*
>
> *I won't lie it took some time but I watched your talk about once a week and then I had the impulse…"*

She had the instinct to get real with herself. She had the desire to assert herself and take control of her life. She had the urge to change. And she did! Not only did she talk to her parents, but she changed her major.

> *"Was accepted to the University of my choice and the course of my choice and am due to go this October. As for my weight, since December I've lost 28lbs from eating healthily, getting into a good exercise routine and it's all down to your 5 second rule.*
>
> *I hope I didn't take up too much of your time, but I really wanted to tell you how much your talk impacted me! I have still got a long way to go but whenever I feel myself slipping I watch your talk again!"*

That's what it takes. It takes courage to do what Alice did. It takes courage to be honest with yourself about what you want. It takes courage to assert yourself—to start. Often, that first step is the hardest. If you fall off the wagon or "slip," you can get back on track. Slipping is normal. There are days when you won't feel like it. Remember, you can take control again. It takes just five seconds.

Just ask Kristin. She says something really important in her Instagram post —"The first step—getting out of bed—is the hardest. But so worth it." No matter how many times you've exercised, starting each day is the hardest part.

kristinsb The first step - getting out of bed - is the hardest. But so worth it when the pedals start to spin. #5secondrule #onthetrainer #teambetty2016 #badassisbeautiful #goproselfie #goprosession #kinetic

Remember when I told you that I wanted you to start experimenting with the Rule by doing the Wake Up Challenge? That's so you can experience "activation energy." It's the force required to start something, and that's exactly what Kristin is referring to. And she's right—it is so worth it. In fact, there's nothing more worth it than learning to push yourself right past your excuses and one step closer to the life, the body, or the future you dream about.

Maybe your health challenge isn't about the gym. Maybe it's about something scarier, like fighting an illness. You aren't alone and you need courage every day to heal, to live, and to stay strong. A lot of people have written about struggling with cancer and setbacks in health, wondering how they can reclaim their courage and strength to fight. The #5SecondRule is a tool that you can use to find the inner strength to face serious illness.

Greg Cheek is one heck of an inspiring guy to follow. Stage three cancer. What did he do? He's run 10 marathons—since his diagnosis! How incredible is that?

Maybe it's not about running marathons. Maybe health for you means being brave enough to get your annual mammogram screening done. When Amy Robach, the host of *Good Morning America*, was asked to have her first-ever mammogram live on-air during Breast Cancer Awareness Month, her initial internal response was *no way, no how*. She didn't have any connection to the disease and didn't want to make it look like she was trying to steal the limelight. Amy turned to Robin Roberts, a fellow anchor and a breast cancer survivor, for advice. After Amy told Robin that she had never had a mammogram, Robin replied:

"Amy, that's the whole point. Listen. Nobody knows better than I do how uncomfortable it can be having people watching you go through something medical. But the power of saving even one life is so remarkable, you'll never regret it. And I can pretty much guarantee it will save a life. Just by you walking into that mammogram and demystifying this test, someone will find out they have cancer who wouldn't have otherwise. Amy, 80% of women who have breast cancer have no family history."

Amy made up her mind right there, in Robin's dressing room, and decided to have the mammogram. She went back on air weeks later to reveal that the screening she had done on live television had saved her life—she had been diagnosed with breast cancer. Amy went through a double mastectomy, eight rounds of chemotherapy, and today is cancer-free.

While Amy didn't use the #5SecondRule in her decision, she got a push from Robin during a critical moment and made a five second decision. Thank goodness she did. You may not be lucky enough to have a work colleague there to push you, but you can always give yourself that push, 5- 4- 3- 2- 1-GO.

Improving your health is all about action. You might not lose as much weight as Charlie, or run marathons like Greg, but you can push yourself to get to the dentist, to exercise, or go to the doctor for a test like a mammogram or prostate screening. When you push yourself just like so many of the people you've just read about, the life that you change will be your own.

Life is about the choices we make. And I have said over and over in this book that you can always choose how you act. If you have goals to get healthier, what you need to do is usually straightforward. Pick a plan to follow, any plan will do— and then 5- 4- 3- 2- 1-GO. The only thing you will need to choose after that is choosing each and every day to DO IT even though, as Anouk said, you "really really really don't feel like it."

I said that what you need to do is simple. I didn't say it would be easy. I promise you, it will be worth it. Exercise and health comes down to one simple rule—you don't have to feel like it. You just have to do it.

Go the extra mile. It's never crowded.

CHAPTER TEN

INCREASE PRODUCTIVITY

> ## "NOTHING WILL WORK UNLESS YOU DO."
>
> ## MAYA ANGELOU

Productivity can be boiled down to one word—FOCUS. There are two types of focus you need to master productivity: **First** the ability to manage distractions so that you can focus moment-to-moment on the task at hand, and **second**, the skill of focusing on what's truly important to you in the big picture, so you don't waste your day on stupid stuff.

We're going to explore both types of focus, take a look at the latest research on the subject, and learn how to use the #5SecondRule to master the skills of focusing your time on what's most important and managing distractions when they pop up.

Get Serious About Managing Distractions

Managing distractions is like following through on health goals. You're never going to feel like it; you just have to make yourself do it. You already know that being addicted to your phone, texting, and answering emails is a distraction…but stopping it feels impossible.

Even though you know you should turn off pop-up alerts, silence your phone, and stop checking email every five minutes, this knowledge doesn't change your behavior. I could bury you with research about how bad this is, but it wouldn't change your behavior. This is where the #5SecondRule comes into play—you don't have to want to do it, you just have to push yourself to do it.

First you must decide that distractions are not good. Interruptions of any sort are the kiss of death for your productivity. Research shows open office spaces are a nightmare for focus. Checking email can become an addiction because of what behavioral researchers call "random rewards." You have to decide that your goals are more important than push notifications. It's that simple.

Then you just remove them. I'm not claiming this is rocket science. I'm also not going to tell you that it's easy. But I promise you that if you use the #5SecondRule, you'll actually do it. When you start to remove distractions and are able to focus on the moment-to-moment things that matter you will have "no idea" how much it will help, as Karen wrote:

> **hendricks_luv** You have no idea how much you have helped me. No idea. Every single day. From the bottom of my heart, Thank you😍

Recently, I was talking about this with my high school-aged daughter Kendall. She loves social media, but would spend so much time on her phone that it was seriously distracting her from her schoolwork. Plus, it was making her feel insecure to constantly compare herself to the social media posts of celebrities and supermodels.

Just like you and me, she knew that social media was making her less productive when she needed to focus on homework. Kendall decided that the best way to manage the distraction of social media would be to get rid of the temptation—so she deleted photo sharing apps Instagram and VSCO from her phone.

In her words:

"After deleting it, it dawned on me how unimportant the stuff is to my life. When these apps were on my phone, it was an involuntary action to click on it and look. Now that the apps are gone, I don't have the urge to look at it ever."

And distractions are not only in the form of technology and social media. Sarah found that her clutter was a major distraction in her life and decided to take action. She used the Rule to beat "emotional" hoarding and 5- 4- 3- 2- 1 and "donated, recycled, sold and also trashed" so much stuff:

 **oneisstarvedfortechnicolor**
I'm using the five second rule to declutter my life. I'm an emotional hoarder and it was becoming problematic. So when I'm clearing through my junk I make my choice in five seconds: and sure enough it works. I've donated, recycled, sold and also trashed a LOT of things in the past few weeks. Now it feels amazing not to be bogged down by useless "stuff".

By clearing through her junk with five second decisions, Sarah now feels "amazing" and is no longer "bogged down." So if you find yourself getting distracted like Kendall was by social media or Sarah was by her surroundings, that's a huge moment of power. You just woke up and now it's time to shake up your environment. 5- 4- 3- 2- 1. Remove the distraction. It really is that simple and the rewards are powerful.

The harder and more powerful thing to do is to master the second type of focus: big picture focus. There's one thing that I've used the #5SecondRule to do that has increased my big picture focus like nothing else—being a "boss" about my mornings.

Own Your Mornings

Taking control of your mornings is a game changer for productivity. The way I did it was to create a morning routine. Alissa found after she implemented her own morning routine, she started to "rule" her days:

> allthethingsetc Ok so I have become a little obsessed with @melrobbinslive I love her message and I am practicing her rules, getting up early (I hate that but I want to love it), eating breakfast (coffee, I don't eat it normally), not touching my phone till after! Clearing my mind. Set intentions and Rule my day!
> #mondays #motivation #melrobbins

Just as Alissa said, when you create a morning routine and follow it, you "set your intentions." And over and over, you'll trigger a chain of events that will shock you.

I owe my morning routine to Duke University professor Dan Ariely. According to Ariely, the first two to three hours of the day are the best hours for your brain, once you fully wake up. So, if you pop out of bed at 6 a.m., your peak thinking and productivity window is 6:30 a.m. to 9 a.m. And so on.

If your household is anything like ours, it's chaos most mornings. Feeding the dog, getting breakfast ready, and guiding three school-ready kids out the door can chew up more than an hour and cut into your peak productivity window. That's why I had to get serious about my mornings if I planned to be the boss of my day—and it started with getting up earlier so that I had time to focus on my big picture goals before the day hijacked me.

Here's how I changed my routine to become a master at focusing on my priorities:

My Daily Routine

1. I get up when the alarm rings.

We went over the importance of this when you learned about the Wake Up Challenge. The alarm rings. I get up. The end. For peak productivity, you should NEVER hit the snooze button. There's actually a neurological reason why, one that I learned while conducting research for this book.

You know that getting a good night's sleep is important for productivity. But I bet you didn't know that **how you wake up is just as important as how you sleep.** Scientists have recently discovered that when you hit the snooze button it has a *negative impact on brain function and productivity* that can last up to four hours! Here's what you need to know.

We sleep in cycles that take about 90 to 110 minutes to complete. About two hours before you wake up, these sleep cycles end and your body starts to slowly prepare to wake up. When your alarm rings, your body is in wakeup mode. If you hit the snooze button and drift back to sleep, you force your brain to start a new sleep cycle that is 90 to 110 minutes long.

When the "snooze" alarm goes off 15 minutes later, the cortical region of your brain, which is the part of the brain responsible for decision-making, attention, alertness, and self-control, is still in the sleep cycle. It won't be able to snap awake— it needs 75 more minutes to finish what that snooze button started.

It can take up to four hours for this "sleep inertia" condition to wear off and for your cognitive functions to return to their full capacity. That's why you feel so darn groggy when you get up after hitting the snooze. It's not because you didn't get enough sleep. It's because once you hit the snooze button, you started a new sleep cycle and then interrupted it. On days when you hit the snooze button, there's no way you're at your best.

So, I'm dead serious about this. The alarm goes off. No snooze button. Get up. Not negotiable.

2. I walk to the bathroom and turn off the alarm.

My husband and I do not have our phones or alarm clocks in our bedroom or on our nightstands. Where is my phone? In the bathroom. Close enough so I can hear the phone ring if someone calls and the alarm ring in the morning. But, far enough so I don't fall to temptation. If my phone is on the nightstand, I will grab it without thinking and stay in bed reading emails. You know you're guilty of the same. If it's in reach, it's easy to grab without thinking. A majority of adults read emails before they get out of bed, and a recent study from Deloitte reports that one-third of adults and one-half of those under the age of 35 actually wake up and check their phones in the middle of the night. By putting my phone/alarm in the bathroom, I'm making it harder to succumb to the habit of reaching for my phone, and I am setting myself up for a good night's sleep.

3. I brush my teeth and focus on the day ahead.

I use the 3 to 5 minutes of time that I spend washing my face and brushing and flossing my teeth to focus my thoughts on what I really want and need to do for ME and MY big-picture goals. This is not a to-do list. This is a "must list." It's a moment when I consciously collect my thoughts and think of one or two things I might not *feel* like doing but that I *must* do today—for my goals, dreams, and business growth. Researchers call these SMART goals (Specific, Measurable, Achievable, Realistic, Timely). I just call them two things that will guarantee forward progress on things that matter to me. It's usually the "crap" I don't feel like doing, just as Morphin described:

 **Morphin**

@melrobbins watched your TED Talk woke up 1 hour earlier and will finally force myself to do some crap I don't feel like doing. Worth it thx

4. I get dressed, make my bed, walk into the kitchen, and pour a cup of coffee.

Have you noticed what I haven't done yet? I haven't looked at my phone or gone online to check email. Why? Because I know that the second I do, I will lose my focus. The moment you check email, read the news or surf social media, someone else's priorities jump in front of yours. Do you think that Bill Gates and Oprah are lying in bed scrolling through social feeds? Nope, and neither should you. You must put yourself first, so do not check email until you plan YOUR day.

5. I write down my 1 to 3 *"musts"* and why they are important.

In my cheapo daily planner that I bought at an office supply store, I jot down the one, two, or three things that I feel I *must* do today—that are for ME. There are a couple of reasons why this is an important step: one, because I am a visual person, and two, according to research by Dominican University of California psychology professor Dr. Gail Matthews, by simply writing down your goals, you are 42% more likely to achieve them.

Having them written in my planner means that I'll see them throughout the day and be reminded to act. Having the "why" statement reminds me of why these goals are important and gives me an added push.

If I put them in my electronic calendar, I'll forget about it. Half the time, I walk into a room and can't remember what I walked in for—so I "stalk myself with my musts" by keeping them written down. When they are in my planner, which is something that I look at throughout the day, I'm cued visually. Seeing my "musts" reminds me to do these tasks. You can do this in a notebook, in your calendar, wherever—just write them down and keep them with you, just like Sharon does:

Sharon
@melrobbins I'm in control of my task list! #5secondrule #ThankYou

6. I plan my day and take 30 before 7:30 a.m.

I plan and often execute the most important "musts" FIRST, before I check my phone or go online and check email. I do this using a tool I call "30 before 7:30 a.m."

I take 30 minutes before 7:30 a.m. to plan out my day. During this time block, I either start working on my two or three musts or I schedule time to get them done later in the day. If I am home, I try to start this planning session at 7:00 a.m. when the last one of our kids leaves for the bus. These 30 minutes are critical to my success.

By setting up your day to make sure that you "focus on the right things," as Jeremy does, you prime yourself to be "much more productive" and successful in accomplishing your goals for the day.

> **jzarghami** @melrobbinslive I've been using the rule so much lately! It has helped me be so much more productive and it helps me focus on the right things. Thank you so much!

The concept of "30 before 7:30 a.m." cannot be done once you walk into the office. You must do this at home or at your favorite coffee shop or on the train or sitting in your car in the parking lot. I'm not kidding. The moment you walk into your office and answer that first email or take that first call, your day is gone.

Professor Sune Carlsson studied how CEOs get so much accomplished. What was the secret of these high-powered executives? They worked at home for 90 minutes because "there was some chance of concentration." At work, they reported being interrupted every 20 minutes. And what did I tell you about interruption? It's the kiss of death to productivity.

Why else is it important to plan and do the most important stuff first thing?

Remember, as Dr. Ariely told us, the first 2 to 3 hours of the day are the best hours for the brain to focus on the tasks or goals that advance your own personal or professional goals. Filling that time with unimportant stuff is stupid.

Answering emails, taking phone calls, and sitting in meetings have a way of taking over your schedule and rarely lead to making major improvements in your life. For your own happiness and to protect the time necessary to focus on the deep work, the first few hours of your day must be grabbed by you, for you. Fight for it.

If you work on two things you consider important, you are making progress on projects that matter—and are winning the long game.

Waking up early and planning out your day has huge benefits. Just ask Mari:

> I loved your TEDxSF Talk and immediately wrote a blog post and started on a book. I've been getting up at 5am for a couple of weeks and enjoying the benefits immensely. I've been writing a journal as a checklist to get my daily rituals done.
>
> The book will summarise the path I followed and the achievements that this brought over the course of a year.

By jumpstarting his mornings with early wakeups (no snooze!), checklists, and rituals, he has been able to take control, set his priorities straight and find time to start working on a new book. I followed up a few weeks later, asking Mari how the morning ritual was going:

> Today is Day#54 for me getting up at (of before) 5am and following a daily ritual. The 5 second rule gets my butt out of bed on the cold mornings and into my 'first thing workout'
>
> Mari

That's amazing, Mari, day #54 of being a boss. Tony did the same and found his "way back into the gym every morning at 5a!":

 **Tony**
@melrobbins since attending your 5 seconds training in MPLS about a month ago I have forced my way back into the gym every morning at 5a!

I know it's hard to get up that early and get right into a workout, but when you 5- 4- 3- 2- 1 to find the activation energy to beat those feelings of resistance, you not only set yourself up to be the boss of your day, but you also activate your greatest self.

7. I plan my quitting time.

Here's something else I learned from research. In addition to planning my day, I also plan the time I will stop working. That's right. Every day, when I start my day, I determine what time I will stop working and hang out with my family. Having a deadline for stopping or redirecting does two things: it makes me more intentional with the time I have and that makes me more productive.

There's a principle called Parkinson's Law—work expands to whatever time you give it. So give your workday a deadline. A deadline is important for stamina and mental health. It forces you to focus and be serious about taking the break from work. It's a break that we all need to be present with our families and give our brains the time to rest, recharge, and reset that they require. I'm not going to lie, I've had to use the rule to force myself 5- 4- 3- 2- 1 to turn off the computer to stop working for the day more often than I would like to admit.

Using this daily routine has helped immeasurably. It is how I put my priorities ahead of putting out daily fires. I feel more in control because I own my actions from the moment the alarm rings. I have more clarity (which helps spot opportunities) because I've defined the 2-3 big picture musts that will move my goals forward.

If I notice myself detouring from my routine or getting distracted, that's a moment of power. I use the Rule, 5- 4- 3- 2- 1 to get back on track. Of course, you can create any routine that works, but if you are looking for a way to start, try mine. Lots of people have found great success adding exercise, meditation, and gratitude lists to their morning routines. Road test them all to see what works best for you.

What I'm telling you is simple, it's obvious, and it works. Customize it so it works for you, but by all means 5- 4- 3- 2- 1 to do it. When you do the work to be the boss of your day, as Christie says, it's a "real game changer." She has achieved the highest rank in her company and is "on fire."

 Christie

I have learned that I can push myself to limits I never thought possible. I have learned it is as simple as 5,4,3,2,1... Thank you Mel Robbins for your talk, a real game changer. I have learned that no matter what you want, if you work hard enough, it will and it can happen! I have met some of the most amazing people that have achieved the highest rank possible within our company and I have learned so many tips and tricks to work my business, my mind is spinning and on fire!

Now it's your turn.

Start before you're ready. Don't prepare, begin.

CHAPTER ELEVEN

END PROCRASTINATION

"TO BEGIN, BEGIN."

WILLIAM WORDSWORTH

The #5SecondRule is an incredible weapon in the fight against procrastination. Before we dig into how to use it, we need to define procrastination, what it is, and what it isn't. In researching this book, I was shocked when I learned what causes procrastination. I had it all wrong!

I was also surprised to learn there are two kinds of procrastination: destructive procrastination, which is when you avoid tasks you need to complete, and productive procrastination, which is an important part of any creative process.

Let's start with the good kind.

Productive Procrastination

If you are working on a creative project or an innovative idea, research shows that procrastination is not only good, but it is also important. The creative process takes time, so when you set a project aside for a few days or weeks, your mind can wander. That extra time spent mental wandering gives you the ability to come up with more creative, "divergent" ideas that enhance your project.

Productive procrastination was a hugely liberating concept for me to learn, especially while struggling to write this book. Before I learned about productive procrastination, I beat myself up constantly because I kept feeling burnt out, I had writer's block, and I thought it meant I was a bad writer, lazy, or incapable. In truth, a creative process of this magnitude just took time.

My mind needed breaks and time to wander. It took me seven months longer than I thought it would to finish and the book is 100 times better for it. If you're not getting the results that you want, give the project some time, go focus your energy somewhere else, and then come back later with fresh eyes.

So, if you are working on a creative project, and you don't have a fixed deadline, it's not procrastination if you let your work sit for a few weeks so you can let you mind wander. It's the creative process. Those fresh new ideas you have as you procrastinate productively will make your work even smarter.

Destructive Procrastination

Destructive procrastination is an entirely different animal. It's when we avoid the work we need to get done and *know* there will be negative consequences. This habit really comes back to bite you in the end.

Every one of us has a pile of stuff we can't seem to get to: updating photo albums, analyzing a spreadsheet, finishing a proposal, cleaning out Dad's house, or plowing through a to-do list that would grow your business. It's anything that we find ourselves deliberately avoiding that really needs to get done.

Evelyn found herself procrastinating and beating herself up: "I have questioned everything about myself for years." She put the Rule into effect and it's been

"AMAZING."

Once she discovered 5- 4- 3- 2- 1-GO, Evelyn was able to push past her questioning and just got things done, impressing even herself.

Mel, I got up yesterday after I put the rule into effect... I have questioned everything about myself for years. I start..I stop..I'm nothing..I'm something..I cleaned my living room, kitchen, dining room, did 7 loads of laundry and I was AMAZING! THAT'S just the beginning! I impressed myself!! I'm signed up..my husband is signed up and I'm ready to move!!!

She probably didn't know why she was procrastinating. Most of us don't. For a long time, everyone believed procrastination meant poor time management skills, a lack of willpower, or lack of self-discipline. Boy, were we wrong. Procrastination is not a form of laziness at all. It's a coping mechanism for stress.

Procrastination and the Connection to Stress

Timothy Pychyl, a psychology professor at Carleton University, has been studying procrastination for more than 19 years. Dr. Pychyl has found that the main thing driving procrastination is not avoiding work. It's avoiding stress. Procrastination is "a subconscious desire to feel good *right now*" so you can feel a little stress relief.

A common mistake we all make is thinking that people make a deliberate choice to procrastinate. In fact, most people who struggle with procrastination tell researchers that they feel like they have no control over it. And they are right, because they don't understand the real reason why we procrastinate.

We procrastinate because we feel stressed out. Here's the catch…you aren't stressed about the work. You are stressed about the bigger stuff: money, relationship problems, or life in general. When you blow off work or studying for 15 minutes of online shopping or watching the highlights of last night's game, you are taking a mini stress-break from the bigger stress you feel overall.

It's like emotional eating for the mind. When you avoid something that feels hard, you get a sense of relief. Plus, when you do something you enjoy, like surfing Facebook or laughing at viral videos, you get a short-term boost of dopamine. The more often that you procrastinate, the more likely you'll repeat the behavior. Here's the problem: While you get a small boost of relief when you watch cat videos, over time the work that you are avoiding builds and that creates more stress in your life.

Scott is an excellent example of this. He wrote to me because he wanted help "getting out of his own head." He shared that everyone close to him has always said, "I'm the only thing that is holding me back." And they are right.

Scott is a PhD student performing research in a physiology lab, he is married, and he and his wife just had their first child who is "the most beautiful baby boy." He described his life like this:

> *"Everything at home is incredible despite **lots of financial stress** which would be expected considering that I'm in school. My issue is that in my daily life, and branching into school/lab work, I have trouble fulfilling obligations which is starting to become a problem. **Basically I put things off continuously until it reaches the point where I've either missed a deadline or it upsets someone.**
>
> **I have very high expectations for myself** and I literally go to sleep every night telling myself that tomorrow is going to be that fresh start that I need and I'm going to tackle everything with tons of energy. But then I fail day after day and that confidence in overcoming this by myself is starting to fade. **Basically I don't feel like I'm living anywhere near my full potential and it's frustrating.**"*

Reading Scott's note, you can see that he's trapped in a vicious cycle of feeling disappointed in himself. I can totally relate because that's how I felt as I was struggling to get out of bed on time. Scott knows what he needs to do (attack the work and get it done), but he can't seem to make himself do it.

Scott's note gives me a chance to explain what's actually going on when you procrastinate. He told us that he and his wife are under "*a lot of financial stress.*" That financial stress doesn't feel good. It also explains the reason why he procrastinates to get temporary relief from the money stress. Remember that when we replace difficult tasks with doing something easier, we get a temporary mood boost and a feeling of control.

It seems counterintuitive, but the reason why Scott keeps blowing off the stuff he needs to do at the lab is because he wants relief from the financial stress he feels in his life.

So how on earth does he stop this? Luckily, there's three simple and research-backed steps. And, the #5SecondRule will help you 5- 4- 3- 2- 1 do them. Whether you are avoiding work like Scott, cleaning like Evelyn, or exercising like @JLosso once was, you can use the Rule to beat procrastination every time.

JLosso

@melrobbins saw you speak this week at LTEN....5-4-3-2-1....I have worked out every day since...

Forgive Yourself

The first thing research tells us: you need to forgive yourself for procrastinating. Seriously. This isn't Kumbaya—this is science.

Remember our expert from Carleton University? Dr. Pychyl co-authored a paper about how students who forgave themselves for procrastinating were less likely to procrastinate on their next test. Sounds silly, but part of the problem that psychologists have uncovered is that procrastinators are really hard on themselves to begin with.

Trishke found that after she was able to forgive herself, she changed her life.

Trishke

The 5 second rule!Go watch @melrobbins It will change ur life,u won't feel sorry4 urself anymore(like I use 2).Reach ur goals,live ur dreams

Instead of beating herself up, she's no longer procrastinating. Amazing!

You may also relate to Ryan, who wrote to me about being in the beginning stages of starting a new business. He said that as much as he wants this venture to work, "it amazes me how hard it is to force myself to spend (time on it) and actually do it due to the fear of failure."

> Just watched your tedx talk! My impulse was to look you up and make a connection with you, so I done it. I'm in the beginning stages of starting a new product related business and was just searching the Internet for validation that I'm doing the right thing by just going for it. I'm not a wealthy person, so as much as I want it to work, it amazes me how hard it is to force myself to spend and actually do it due to the fear of failure. You talk definitely motivated me and win or lose, atleast I'm doing something! Thanks for doing what you do, we are grateful.

I love what he said at the end: "Win or lose, at least I'm doing something!" It takes a lot of bravery to be able to get honest with yourself and admit how hard it is to focus on what you need to do.

Another perfect example is our PhD student in the lab, Scott. Remember what he wrote? He said he has "very high expectations for myself." Every time he procrastinates he feels shame and guilt. Those negative feelings then create even more stress for Scott as his "confidence in overcoming this by myself is starting to fade," which causes him to feel even more stress and procrastinate even more.

So, let's apply this advice to Scott. Step number one, stop the cycle by forgiving yourself. Scott, you've got to take five seconds, 5- 4- 3- 2- 1 forgive yourself for upsetting people, falling behind, and not working to your full potential. If you can recognize that your stress about finances are driving the procrastination at the lab, now you've got a chance to assert yourself and take control. By the way, you want to take control so you can achieve your goals. And that person you hope to become can help you right now.

That leads us to Step 2.

What Would the Future You Do?

Allow me to explain. Dr. Pychyl's team has been doing a lot of research on our "present self" versus our "future self." Our "future self" is the person that we want to become. Interestingly, research proves that when you can picture the "Future You," it gives you the objectivity to push yourself in the present moment. In experiments when researchers show people their own pictures digitally aged, they're more likely to save for retirement. I guess that's an explanation for why vision boards work. They help you envision the Future You and that is a great coping mechanism for the stress you experience today as the Present You. So, Scott, create a vision board or a mental image of what your life looks like when all this grad school stress is behind you and you are Professor Scott. The moment you feel yourself procrastinating, just ask yourself, *What would "Professor Scott" do?*

This leads us to Step 3.

Get Started with the #5SecondRule

Finally, once you understand the source of procrastination, Dr. Pychyl's favorite advice is, "Just get started." He's not the only one talking about the importance of starting. One of the most powerful ways to create new habits, according to researchers, is to "create a starting ritual." There's no better starting ritual than the #5SecondRule. Now that I understand the science of all this, I can explain why "just get started" works.

- If procrastinating is a habit, you have to replace the bad behavior pattern (avoidance) with a new positive one (getting started).

- The moment you feel yourself hesitate, doing easier tasks, or avoiding hard work, use the Rule, 5- 4- 3- 2- 1 push yourself to start the important thing you need to do.

- Getting started takes us back to our engineer at CISCO and the concept of a "locus of control." Procrastination makes you feel like you have no control over yourself. When you assert yourself and just get started, you are taking control of the moment and your life.

Daniela feels "empowered" and "capable" when she puts the Rule into practice, showing us that the benefits of beating procrastination expand beyond work and into the more important areas of improving "my relationship with myself."

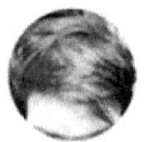 My relationship with myself has improved. I trust myself more. I feel empowered and capable. It has become my mantra. DO SOMETHING NOW. (Thanks Mel!)

As I explain throughout the book, exerting effort with 5- 4- 3- 2- 1 switches the gears in your mind and allows the prefrontal cortex to help you get started. Each time you use the Rule, it'll get easier and easier to stop procrastinating and just start. Just as Sy found out, telling yourself to "just make the call, reply the email, finish the stupid job…" and start is the secret to completing anything important:

Sy

Dear Mel I am writing to say thank you. It is about your presentation on TEDx talk. I watched it about few months ago. After that, I am keep telling myself "Just make the call, reply the email, finish the stupid job..I don't like it but it helps me to get what I want." I am glad that I have done a huge project after getting this habit. Thank you so much for that amazing presentation! :)

Even though she doesn't like doing it, she's formed the habit of taking action anyway—and has completed a huge project with this mindset and will "get what I want."

In Scott's case, back in the lab, he can use the Rule to countdown 5- 4- 3- 2- 1 and push himself to work for a short interval of time. Now that he realizes the source of his procrastination (financial stress), he has forgiven himself (extremely important step). And once he is picturing the future Dr. Scott, he can start counting to assert control, physically move to his desk, and begin working. When he finds himself getting off track, he can countdown 5- 4- 3- 2- 1 again. The Rule makes it easier to just GET GOING, something that will help Scott gain control of his work and feel better equipped to deal with his other financial stresses head on.

Andre also used the Rule to push past procrastination and act on his goals. Andre is 16 years old, but he's already learning how to beat procrastination and is starting to write a book! He said that he always had excuses: that he wasn't "ready, too busy, not smart enough." The Rule helped him to "get past those excuses" and now he is taking action on his book.

 Andre

I began to rely on an urge to act on my ideas, which led to my involvement in Be Z Change (a club with a focus in community service) which I am now president of. I also took action in reaching out to colleges and acting on my immediate academic goals. Many of my recent achievements were possible because I chose to engage in that idea within the five seconds I had the impulse. My objective now is to write a book; an impulse I had never taken the time to act on because I always had an excuse: I wasn't ready, I was too busy, I'm not smart enough. This rule helped me to get passed those excuses by taking the initiative to simply write down my goal and build on it. Every time I saw that sticky note about focusing my creativity on writing a book, I took a step, I tried something. It changed my life.

Andre shows us that at any age and with any goal we have the power to own ourselves, look inside, take "a step," try "something," and "change my life." The reason why just starting is so important is because you'll also be tapping into what researchers call "the progress principle," which describes the phenomenon that forward progress of any kind, including small wins, boosts our mood and increases our happiness and productivity levels.

On top of that, once you start a project, you'll have triggered a mechanism in your brain to cue you to keep at it. As I mentioned earlier researchers have found out that the brain remembers unfinished tasks better than finished ones. Once you start, your mind will keep nudging you to finish.

I also told you that my snooze button habit was a form of procrastination. Now I understand why. It gave me momentary relief from the larger stresses in my life. That's why I hit it. When I reflect back, I see now that I broke the habit by creating a "starting ritual"—the #5SecondRule. My snooze button habit got replaced with a positive new one: counting 5- 4- 3- 2- 1 and then standing up and starting the day. Seven years later, I still count backwards to launch myself out of bed every single morning.

So, in sum, here's how you can most effectively use the #5SecondRule to beat procrastination: use it to make yourself start. Start small. Attack what you are avoiding for just 15 minutes at a time. Then, take a break and watch a few cat videos. And for crying out loud, give yourself a break for blowing things off until now. You're only human.

All of this stuff is common sense. You eat the elephant (in the room) one bite at a time. What we are learning over and over in this book is that unless you beat the feelings that trigger your bad habits, and you push yourself to just get started, you'll never change.

You'll either find a way or you'll find an excuse.

PART4
COURAGE CHANGES YOUR MIND

HOW TO BECOME THE HAPPIEST PERSON YOU KNOW

In the next three chapters, you'll learn the step-by-step approach to how you can use the #5SecondRule in combination with some recent research-based strategies to beat fear, stop worrying, manage or cure anxiety, and change the way you think.

If you've seen me on TV as a commentator for CNN or read my columns in *SUCCESS* magazine, it's easy to assume that I was born with the confidence of a warrior. That assumption only gets strengthened when you watch my YouTube videos, my TEDx Talk, or experience me live on stage. Yes, I am confident now, but I was not born this way. For most of my adult life, I was a loud-mouthed extrovert who was plagued by deep insecurity. Confidence is a skill I've built over the years by practicing acts of everyday courage.

What a lot of people don't know about me is that I have suffered from anxiety for more than twenty-five years. I had debilitating post-partum depression when our first daughter Sawyer was born and I couldn't be left alone with her for the first two months. I have taken Zoloft to control my panic attacks for nearly two decades. The struggle with my thoughts has been real and, at times, terrifying.

When I first discovered the Rule, I used it to change my behavior. The Rule worked wonders, and as acting with everyday courage became second nature, my confidence grew stronger. However, anxiety never disappeared. It was there simmering beneath the surface. I focused on learning to live with it, managing it, and making sure I didn't let it boil over into full blown panic.

About four years ago, I started to wonder if I could use the #5SecondRule to change more than my physical behavior. I wondered if I could change my thoughts. I had seen the effects it had on other habits—so why not try to break the mental habit of anxiety, panic, and fear? They are patterns that we repeat after all. They are just habits.

I started using the Rule to change the way that my mind worked. I began by using the Rule to break the habit of worrying. As I mastered that skill, I used the Rule to control my anxiety and beat my fear of flying. It worked.

As I write this sentence, I can tell you—I have cured myself of anxiety. I haven't taken Zoloft in years and am panic attack-free. I no longer have a habit of worrying. And my fear of flying? Gone. Learning to take control of my mind, direct my thoughts, and dismantle fear has been the single greatest thing I have ever done to improve the quality of my life. I almost never feel worried. And the rare times that I do, I just, 5- 4- 3- 2- 1 and direct my mind towards the solutions rather than worrying about the problems. I have transformed my mind using the Rule and I am the happiest and most optimistic that I have ever been. My mind is working for me instead of against me.

Now, it's your turn.

First, you'll learn how to break the addiction to worrying and negative self-talk using the #5SecondRule, the science of habits, and the power of gratitude.

Second, you'll dive into the subject of anxiety and panic. You'll learn what it is and what it isn't. And I will give you the step-by-step method for how you can interrupt, reframe, and eventually eliminate anxiety from your own life.

Finally, you'll learn a proven strategy for how you can beat any fear. Using my fear of flying as an example, you'll learn how to use the Rule with "anchor thoughts" to prevent fear from taking over your mind.

Everything you are about to learn is so simple and powerful that you can even teach it to your kids.

Life is amazing.

And then it's awful.

And then it's amazing again.

And in between the amazing and the awful,
it's ordinary and mundane and routine.
Breathe in the amazing, hold on through
the awful, and relax and exhale
during the ordinary. That's just living.

Heartbreaking, soul-healing, amazing,
awful, ordinary life. And it's
breathtakingly beautiful.

-LR Knost

CHAPTER TWELVE

STOP WORRYING

"THINK OF THE BEAUTY STILL LEFT AROUND YOU AND BE HAPPY."

ANNE FRANK

More than any other change, ending your habit of worrying will create the single biggest positive impact in your life. Believe it or not, you were taught how to worry. As a kid, you heard your parents worrying constantly *"Be careful,"* *"Wear a hat or you'll catch a cold,"* and *"Don't sit so close to the TV."* As adults, we spend way too much time and energy worrying about things that we can't control or that could go wrong. When you get to be near the end of your life, you'll wish you hadn't.

Dr. Karl Pillemer is a professor of Human Development at Cornell University and is the founder of the Legacy Project. He has met with 1,200 senior citizens to discuss the meaning of life. He was "shocked" to learn that most people near the end of their lives had the same regret: **I wish I hadn't spent so much of my lifetime worrying.** Their advice was "devastatingly simple and direct: worry is an enormous waste of your precious and limited lifetime."

You can stop worrying. And the #5SecondRule will teach you how. Worrying is a default setting that your mind goes to when you aren't paying attention. The key is catching yourself when you drift into worry, and then regaining mental control by using the Rule. Here's an example.

My husband recently got his motorcycle license and just bought a small, used motorcycle. Yesterday, I was sitting inside the house and noticed him on the bike pulling out of the driveway. As he drove down the road, I noticed that my mind immediately started to drift toward worry.

I started worrying about whether or not he would get hit by a car, become a statistic, and if I would soon get a call from the police telling me that he's been in an accident. The worry hijacked me within five seconds. That fast. And you know what? My worrying about it won't keep him safe and it won't prevent an accident. As one 83-year-old in the study said, my worrying "won't solve anything." It will just put me on edge for the entire time Chris is out riding his motorcycle—which robs me of enjoying the present moment.

As soon as I catch myself worrying, I use the Rule, 5- 4- 3- 2- 1 and I think of something more positive—like the thought of him smiling as he drives down the road.

The funny thing is that Chris is also a huge cyclist. He competes in triathlons and is out on the road taking 40 to 50 mile training rides by himself all the time. I never worry about that. But here I am worrying about the motorcycle he is driving down our road at 10 miles per hour. Could something go wrong? Of course it could. But it usually doesn't.

When you start to use the Rule to end worrying, you'll be amazed by how often your mind just drifts to something negative. Mine does it every day. It really sucks. And each day, I fight against it. There are some days that I have to use the Rule a dozen or more times to control my thoughts. Just the other day I caught myself drifting into worry over and over again.

Our daughters were returning home from a service trip in Peru and throughout the day, I caught my mind drifting to thoughts of plane crashes, missed flights, falling off a cliff in the Andes, bus accidents, lost bags, and the girls being stranded at the airport. The girls were fine, and without the Rule I would have ruined my day. Each time I caught my mind drifting to a bad thought, I would say to myself "oh no you don't…" and just point it to a thought that made me smile—like the girls talking a million miles an hour that night in the kitchen as they told us about the trip.

Feelings of Love Often Trigger Worry

Another thing that has surprised me about worry is just how subtle it is and how fast it can seize control of you. I've been surprised by how often I start to worry the moment that I feel happiness or love.

This spring, it happened to me as I was looking at our 17-year-old daughter. I had this incredible moment when my heart just suddenly swelled up and I felt a tidal wave of love wash over me. And then, without warning, all these worries flooded into my mind and stole the moment. All I felt was fear.

We were at the mall. Sawyer was trying on dresses for her high school prom. It had been a long afternoon. We were on our third dress store, and she had easily tried on more than 40 dresses—and she hated every last one of them. Telling her she looked amazing only made her mood worse.

I was in the dressing room with her, putting the rejects back on the hangers and handing her the next gown to try on. I started panicking that we'd never find one that she liked. I handed her another one to try on and said, "Let's just bang through these next three and then get out of here." I stepped out of the dressing room to give her some space and called Chris.

Suddenly she called out to me, "Mom. Can you come in here?"

I tried to read her voice but couldn't tell if she was crying, frustrated, needing help with a stuck zipper, or something else. I cracked open the door. She had on a floor length gown and I could see her reflection in the mirror and she looked, in a word, stunning. It was perfect. The dress was peach and had beautiful flowy side panels that were pink. It was everything she had wanted—no sparkles, no lace, an open back, and a bright color. Our eyes caught in the mirror.

"What do you think, Mom?"

I could feel the tears coming. When she was an infant, I remember experiencing that same tidal wave of emotion that can wash over you when you love someone so much. In the middle of the night, I'd wake up to go check in on her, and there standing alone in her nursery, watching her sleep on her back with her arms raised up above her head, I'd get hit with this tidal wave of love—and just marvel at my ability to love something so much. It felt like my heart might burst.

That's what I felt standing outside the dressing room in the mall. I just felt love. And then, the worries rushed in and stole the moment from me. Without warning, I was thinking about her heading off to college, getting married, being a new mom, living far away from me, time passing, getting older, and my life being over. My life flashed before me. Time was racing by and for a fleeting moment, I felt I was losing her. I felt overwhelmed with sadness and loss and my eyes swelled with tears.

Sawyer saw me getting emotional, and thought it was because of the dress. "Ah, Mom. Don't cry. You'll make me cry." But I was crying because of how scared I was to see her grow up. I was crying because time was passing too fast and I wanted life to slow down. Worry robbed me of all the joy in that moment. It took me away from Sawyer and into a dark place in my head. Instead of just being present and in awe of my beautiful daughter, I felt afraid.

That's how worries and fear hijack your mind and rob you of the magic and wonder in your life. Brené Brown observed this exact phenomenon in her research for her best-seller *Daring Greatly*. She found that feeling a worst-case scenario in moments of joy (such as not being able to enjoy a hug with your child without worrying about something bad happening to him) is an amazingly common phenomenon. And why is it so hard for us to soften into joy? "Because we're trying to beat vulnerability to the punch," says Dr. Brown.

When your mind takes you somewhere sad, dark, doubtful, or negative, you don't have to go with it. I love what Hein wrote to me: "99.999% of the time, it has always been a fake reality that I had created in my head."

 Since I saw your first show on Ted, I've come to realize how big an enemy my bad inner voice has been to not only my self confidence, but more so my ability to move forward and grow my self identity. Every decision and turn has been shaded by self doubt and concerns for what others would think. 99.999% of the time, it has always been a fake reality that I had created in my head. My biggest challenge has, and always will be, to stop worrying what others think of me. It makes no difference. Cheers! Thanks for your great motivations!

When you find your inner voice becoming an "enemy," as Hein and I have experienced, it's important to "stop worrying" and recognize that in those 5 seconds, you can reclaim control.

I started to silently counting to myself, "5- 4- 3-..." and as I counted, I could feel the fear lowering inside by body. Counting yanked me out of my head and planted me in the present moment. It switched gears from worry to focus. I was not going to let my brain rob me of this experience with my daughter. I was not going to allow the habit of worrying to derail me from being in the present and taking a mental photograph.

Then I asked myself two simple questions: *"What am I grateful for in this moment? What do I want to remember?"* When you ask that simple question, you impact your brain at a biological level. In order to respond you have to take stock of your life, relationships, and work and search for an answer in the moment.

It forces you to focus on the positive aspects of your life. As soon as you think about what you are grateful for, you'll start feeling grateful instead of worried. The answer to the question was clear to me. I was grateful to have such an incredible young woman as my daughter. And after three hours of drama, I was also grateful she found a dress.

Katie is also using the Rule to reflect on what she is grateful for and to control her worries:

I saw you in California at the kyani convention. I almost didn't go on that trip. I was riddled with anxiety and guilt leaving my five year old daughter. I'm also going through a divorce. But I went..and I met you. And your a huge inspiration to me. And I used the five second rule before I even knew there was one by pushing myself to go. I cried everyday while I was away.

I'm still using it daily in my life to workout..to not be sad..to be more grateful and no to hold off on my divorce..because we just aren't sure and that's ok. I'm learning that nothing is perfect in life. So thank you.

Katie

"Nothing" in life is perfect. Nothing at all. But you can use 5- 4- 3- 2- 1 to quiet the mental chatter and learn to appreciate all of the small moments like feeling grateful for your daughter.

Feeling grateful doesn't just feel good. According to neuroscientist Alex Korb, it changes your brain chemistry by activating the brainstem region that produces dopamine. With my worries gone, I took a deep breath and stepped into the dressing room to move closer to her and put my hand on her shoulder. Our eyes met in the mirror.

"Well? What do you think, Mom?"

"I think Luke is going to have a heart attack. You look absolutely gorgeous."

It's okay to be scared. Being scared means you're about to do something really, really brave.

CHAPTER THIRTEEN

END ANXIETY

"RULE YOUR MIND, OR IT WILL RULE YOU."

HORACE

Anxiety is what happens when your habit of worrying spirals out of control. As a lifelong anxiety sufferer, I know all too well the grip it can hold on you and how scary it can feel. I also know how to beat it. Using the #5SecondRule in combination with a strategy called "reframing" is the answer.

The key to beating anxiety is understanding it. If you can catch it right as it kicks in and reframe it, you'll stabilize your thoughts before your mind escalates it into full blown panic. And over time, as you use the #5SecondRule over and over, your anxiety will weaken and become what it started—out as simple worries. As you just learned, the habit of worry is easy to break.

I think I was born anxious. As a child, my parents said I had a "nervous stomach" and I worried about everything. I was that kid at camp who was so homesick she had to go home early. As a college student, my face would turn as red as a tomato when I got called on. I relied on liquid courage to talk to hot guys at parties because without alcohol I'd get stress hives on my neck.

The panic attacks started in my early twenties, when I began law school. A panic attack feels like you're about to have a heart attack and can happen for two reasons: one, because you have something scary to do (public speaking, facing an ex, getting on airplane), or two, for no reason at all.

If you've never had a panic attack, here's the best way to describe them: it's when your mind and body have a "near miss" experience that's totally out of context. Allow me to explain using a really simple analogy.

Normal Panic vs. Panic Attacks

There will be tons of times in your life when you will panic and it will be completely normal. Let's say you are driving a car and are about to change lanes on the highway. Suddenly, out of nowhere, a car races by you and cuts you off, you swerve to get out of the way but they nearly miss you. When a "near miss" happens on the highway you feel a surge of adrenaline race through your body. Your heart races. Your breath speeds up. Your cortisol surges. Your body goes into a state of hyper-alertness so you can take control of the car. You might even get a little sweaty.

As soon as your body freaks out, it triggers your mind to find a reason why your body is so agitated. In this example on the highway, your brain knows you almost got in a car crash and that's why your body freaked out.

When your mind has an explanation for why your body just freaked out, it won't escalate the anxiety. Your mind will allow your body to calm down because it knows the "danger" has passed. Your life will go back to normal, and you'll be a little more cautious when you change lanes next time.

When you have a panic attack, that same "near miss" sensation rushes your mind and body, without any warning and with no preceding event. You'll be standing in your kitchen, pouring a cup of coffee and out of nowhere you have a sudden surge of adrenaline race through your body just like what happened when that car nearly missed you on the highway.

Your heart races. Your breath speeds up. You might get a little sweaty. Your cortisol surges. Your body goes into a state of hyper awareness. Now that your body is in an aroused state, your mind is going to race to try understand why. If you don't have a legitimate reason why, your mind will think you must be in actual danger. Your mind will go prehistoric on you and escalate the fear, thinking that danger is imminent.

As your heart starts to race, your mind races for an explanation so it can make sense of what's happening to your body and decide how to protect you. *Maybe I'm having a heart attack. Maybe I don't want to get married next month, after all. Maybe I'm getting fired...maybe I'm dying.*

If your mind can't find a suitable explanation, your brain will make the anxiety worse so that you will want to physically run away from the situation and leave the room. If you've ever seen someone have a panic attack, they freak out, dart around, have scattered thoughts, a "deer in the headlights" look, and suddenly "have to leave the room." It's a vicious cycle and one I was trapped in for years.

For a long time, I understood neither the difference between normal panic and panic attacks, nor the role that my mind was playing in escalating my anxiety. I went to therapists and tried all kinds of cognitive techniques to try to stop myself from panicking. It got so bad that I became afraid of the panic attacks themselves, and that fear, of course, just made me have more panic attacks.

Finally, I just medicated myself with Zoloft (a miracle drug). Zoloft worked wonders for me—for almost two decades. And if you are in a hole you can't climb out of, get professional help (and possibly drugs). While not a substitute for therapy, they can be life changing.

I assumed that I would just take Zoloft for the rest of my life. And then we had kids and all three of them started to struggle with their own form of anxiety. It was beyond mere worrying. The anxiety was impacting their lives—they stopped doing sleepovers, slept on the floor of our bedroom, and were worried about everything. Oakley called his panicky state "Oliver" and our daughter Sawyer called her anxiety a "What-if Loop." She once turned to me and said:

"It's like there's this "What-if Loop" in my head and once I start thinking about all the "What-ifs" I get stuck thinking about all the "What-ifs" and I can't get out of it because there are always "What-ifs."

I knew how scary it was to suffer from it, and it was downright heartbreaking to see our kids struggling and afraid. It was very eye-opening and frustrating trying to help them deal with their anxiety because nothing worked. We went to specialists and tried all kinds of techniques. We set up games with prizes for them to "face their fears." It just seemed to get worse.

I came off Zoloft so I could face my own anxiety head on without the help of drugs. I wanted to understand it better and figure out how to beat it—so I could help my kids figure out ways to beat theirs. Here's what I learned.

Trying To Calm Down Does Not Work

I've spent countless hours with therapists who have told me and the kids to just "change the channel" and think about something else. That works if you are merely worried, but on its own, that strategy doesn't work for full-blown anxiety. And there's a reason. When you feel anxious, you are in a state of physical agitation. When you tell a person to calm down, you are asking someone to go from 60 mph to 0 mph. It's like trying to stop a freight train by throwing a boulder in front of it; it'll jump the tracks.

A study in the journal *Behavior Research and Therapy* showed that people who *naturally try to suppress their unwanted thoughts* end up being more distressed by said thoughts. That's right, when you try to tell yourself to just calm down, you make the anxiety worse because you are fighting against it! When you understand how panic works, what it is, and the role your brain has in making it worse, you can beat it.

There are two strategies that work incredibly well together: Using the #5SecondRule to assert control over your mind and then reframing the anxiety as excitement so that your brain doesn't escalate it and your body can calm down. Here's how you do it.

Excitement and Anxiety Feel the Same In Your Body

I first used this "reframing strategy" as a public speaker. I get a lot of questions about public speaking and specifically how did I get over my fears and nerves about public speaking. My answer always surprises people: I have never gotten over my fears and nerves; I just use them to my advantage.

I speak for a living. A lot. In 2016, I was named the most-booked female speaker in America—98 keynotes in one year. Amazing. Do I get nervous? Absolutely. Every single time. But here's the trick: I don't call it "nerves." I call it "excitement" because **physiologically anxiety and excitement are the exact same thing**. Let me say that again. Fear and excitement are the exact same thing in your body. The only difference between excitement and anxiety is what your mind calls it. Like the "near miss" example. If your brain has a good explanation for why your body is freaking out, it won't escalate things.

The first time I ever really gave a legitimate speech was that TEDx Talk in San Francisco. I remember standing backstage listening to one PhD after another PhD give their talks, thinking to myself, "This is the dumbest thing I've ever gotten myself into. I am going to sound like a complete moron compared to these smart people."

My palms were sweaty. My heart was racing. My face was hot. My armpits were dripping like Niagara Falls. My body was preparing for ACTION! It was getting ready to do something. But I told myself that I was nervous. I labeled all those sensations as a sign that something bad was about to happen and the nerves got worse.

Want to know something wild? Six years and hundreds of speeches later…I still feel the EXACT same things in my body back stage. My palms sweat. My heart races. My face gets hot. My arm pits start dripping. Physiologically, I'm in a state of arousal. I'm about to go into ACTION and my body is getting ready. I feel the exact same thing as fear, I just channel it in a positive direction.

The more speeches I give, the more comfortable and confident I became about what I was saying, but as I gained confidence in my ability I noticed that the feelings in my body didn't disappear. That's when it dawned on me that maybe this was just my body's way to get ready to do something cool. So, I started telling myself that I was getting excited; instead of calling it nervousness.

Say You're Excited

I never knew my "trick" had some serious science behind it. It's called "anxiety reappraisal." Reframing your anxiety as excitement really works. It is as simple as it is powerful. Harvard Business School professor Alison Wood Brooks has conducted study after study to prove that it not only works to lower anxiety—it actually makes you perform better in math tests, speaking, and so forth!

In a nutshell, since anxiety is a state of arousal, it's much easier to convince your brain that all those nervous *feelings* are just excitement rather than to try to calm yourself down. When using this technique in experiments ranging from singing karaoke to giving a speech on camera to taking a math test, participants who said "I'm excited" did better in every single challenge than those participants who said "I'm anxious." Reframing your nervous into enthusiasm works, just as Suzi did. She used the #5SecondRule to 5- 4- 3- 2- 1 and kept "that feeling" in her stomach from stopping her:

 Suzi Helmlinger My husband and I are planning to get out of our comfort spot in a big way. He is going to retire soon and we are looking into moving across country to the East Coast. Every time I get "that feeling" in my stomach (you know the one, fear of change), I remember the 5 second rule and make a list of stuff I have to do and check them off one by one. It's taking us a little closer to our dream. Thank you for your inspiration.
Like · Reply · Message

Now, here's the catch about telling yourself *"I'm excited"*—it doesn't actually lower the feelings surging through your body. It just gives your mind an explanation that empowers you. That way the nervous feelings do not escalate. You stay in control and the agitation in your body will start to calm down as you begin to move.

The next time you have a panic attack while making coffee, experience stage fright, have pre-game jitters, or are worrying about a big exam or a job interview, use the #5SecondRule and this new research to beat your anxiety.

As soon as you feel the anxiety take over your body, take control of your mind, 5- 4- 3- 2- 1 just start telling yourself "I'm so excited" and push yourself to move forward.

This is what J. Greg did when he reframed his feelings in order to beat anxiety:

J. Greg Morrison
View Profile

I have reframed this hesitation as an opportunity to get going on my work in those 5 seconds even though i don't feel like it. I have allowed this 'not feeling like it' to become a full blown anxiety disorder and I truly think that your talks have helped me find a way to get unstuck. Finally!!! So, thank you for helping me to reframe these feelings of never feeling like it as 'normal" rather than 'neurotic'.

The physical impact (the push) is critical and it begins with counting. Exerting yourself allows your prefrontal cortex to take control and focus you on a positive explanation. When you first start using this strategy you might have to repeat it 27 times in one hour. The first time our 11-year-old used it to beat his anxiety about sleeping over at a friend's house, he said "I'm excited to sleep over" over and over for the entire six-mile drive ... bless his little heart.

When I pulled into Quinn's driveway, I put the car in park and said, "How are you doing?" He responded, "My heart is still racing and my stomach feels funny, but I'm excited to sleep over." That was six months ago. His anxiety about sleepovers is gone. He's now actually excited. And that's the power of this tool: It truly works.

"You are braver than you believe, stronger than you seem, and smarter than you think."

-AA Milne

CHAPTER FOURTEEN

BEAT FEAR

> "COURAGE, DEAR HEART."
>
> C.S. LEWIS

Fear will make you do nutty things. One of my greatest fears in life used to be dying in a fiery plane crash. When I had to get on a plane, I used to be a complete weirdo. I had all these superstitions about flying. First, I would scan the boarding area looking for women with small babies, men or women in uniform, priests, nuns, wheelchairs, off-duty pilots catching a ride home, or just generally kind-looking people. Then, I would tell myself that God wouldn't let the plane go down with these nice folks onboard. That would assuage me until I got on the plane. Then every bump or sound the plane made on the taxi out to the runway made my heart race and chest tighten.

Take off was the worst. By the time the wheels left the tarmac, I was usually in a full state of panic. I'd close my eyes and visualize an explosion, terrorists, my row getting sucked out of the plane, or the plane just dropping from the sky. I'd squeeze the arm rest and could barely breathe. If the captain spoke to us over the loudspeaker my fear index would cut in half. I didn't relax until the seat belt lights turned off, which was my sign that the pilots believed it was safe to move about the cabin. In my mind, this meant that the immediate threat of death by plane crash was over.

I cured myself of my fear of flying, using the #5SecondRule and a specific form of anxiety reappraisal that I call "anchor thoughts." And you can use the Rule the exact same way with any fear. Zahara did so with her fear of flying "and it worked!"

 Zahara Khan P.S. I could so relate to your anxieties about flying that you shared at #pmilim in San Diego! Thought I was the only one who dreaded anout their seat being blown in an airplane accident 😫 Stopped watching 'Air crash investigation' and 'Seconds before disaster' for this reason. My friend's advice in 2011 and your 5 second rules helped 👍

Unlike · Reply · Message · 👍 2

 Rizwan Massani Are you flying again?
Like · Reply · Message

 Zahara Khan Already did. Tried 5 secs rule this time and it worked 👍
Like · Reply · Message · 👍 1

Here's how I did it. It's the same technique that I spoke about to Zahara.

Create an Anchor Thought

First, before any trip, I come up with my "anchor thought." This is a thought that is relevant to the trip that I am taking and will anchor me if fear sets in. I start by thinking about the trip, where I am flying to, and what I am excited to do once I get there.

If I am heading to see friends in Driggs, Idaho, my anchor thought might be climbing Table Top mountain. If I'm traveling home to Michigan, I might think about the moment we pull into the driveway of my parents' house and my kids run out of the car to hug my folks or of taking a nice walk along Lake Michigan with my mom. If I'm heading to a meeting in Chicago, I'll think about getting a delicious dinner with a client. Once I have a specific image in mind, the rest is very easy.

This use of the #5SecondRule is a form of what researchers call "If, Then" planning. It's a way to keep yourself in control by creating a backup plan in advance. Plan A is not to get nervous.

But i I do get on the plane and start to feel nervous, **the** I have my Plan B: I'll use the #5SecondRule and my anchor thought to beat my fear of flying. Studies show that this kind of If-Then planning can boost your success rates by almost 3 times.

On the Plane

The moment I notice something that makes me nervous, whether that be an alarming sound, turbulence, a climb that seems to be taking too long, weather that looks ominous, or a bad vibe from a passenger next to me, my fears can be easily triggered because my pattern of thinking is so ingrained. When this happens, I start to count 5- 4- 3- 2- 1 to flush the fear out of my head, activate my prefrontal cortex and pull myself into the present moment.

Then, I force myself to anchor on the specific images of where I am flying to and I think to myself about how excited I am to walk on the beach with my mom, have dinner with a client in Chicago, or climb Table Top Mountain with my buddies.

These anchoring images are powerful reminders of a simple truth…if I am sitting in a restaurant in Chicago having dinner with my clients tonight, or walking the beach in Michigan tomorrow morning with my mom, or arriving home in time to make the girls' lacrosse game, obviously the plane didn't crash and I have nothing to worry about. Most important, I give my mind the context it is looking for—so that it doesn't escalate the fear. As I think about the anchor thought, my body calms down.

By using this technique over and over again, I cured my fear of flying. And by using, I mean using it over and over. It will get easier and easier until suddenly, you won't be afraid anymore. You'll have trained your mind to default to the positive: excitement about what you are about to do instead of the fear. Dana was able to use this technique successfully and she's never "been so calm when flying."

 Dana Siemsen Smith I loved watching you at the Kyäni convention! I used your 5-4-3-2-1 method on the plane yesterday and it worked! I don't think I've ever been so calm when flying!! Thank you!! Your words were inspirational and uplifting!!!!!

And Fran put it to use on the flight home immediately after learning the technique at a conference in Dallas and it made "a world of difference."

Fran

Hi! Thank you! I do have a story.

I've always hated flying and avoid it. Nerium Get Real was in Dallas, and since we live in MD, we had to fly. I was on the verge of a panic attack the entire flight! I was so upset that I got in other people's nerves. lol. Fast forward to you speaking at get real. OMG! It made a world of difference flying home. Every time I felt the panic I used your 5 second rule and halfway through the flight, I was looking out the window and taking pictures! I can't believe how much I was missing by being afraid!

That was proof enough for me, and it's worked in other areas as well.

I love what Fran said at the end of her note: "I can't believe how much I was missing by being afraid!" She's right and it's heartbreaking. I realized the same thing —I was robbing myself of joy, opportunity, and magic every single day because I was living with fear. It doesn't have to be that way. In five seconds flat, you can take control. You can beat fear.

Today, I am never nervous or afraid when I board a plane. Occasionally, if we hit rough turbulence, I'll break out the Rule so that I don't drive my fingernails into the arm of the person sitting next to me.

However, I still use this technique when I face other fears. Before a negotiation or a difficult conversation, for example, I'll create an anchor thought of the conversation or the negotiation going really well. Specifically, I might picture someone hugging me or thanking me for "having the conversation" or toasting the deal with my business partner at our favorite bar.

That thought keeps me grounded, present, and powerful. When you enter a conversation managing a fear, you can't be your best because part of your mind is busy trying to manage that fear in real time. When you have an anchor thought, it allows you to disappear the fear the moment that you notice your mind drift to it.

Remember, even though your fears and your habits can hijack you in five seconds, you can take back control just as quickly and "continue to do so" forever.

 Claudia Granados Thank you, you have helped so many of us face our fears!!! I've already used the 5-4-3-2-1 method, and will continue to do so! Forever grateful!!!

Master your mind and anything is possible.

PART5
COURAGE CHANGES EVERYTHING

HOW TO BECOME THE MOST FULFILLED PERSON YOU KNOW

We're nearing the end of the book. You've learned the story of the Rule, you understand the concept of everyday courage, and you've covered the more tactical uses of the #5SecondRule to change behavior and change your mind. You're now ready to dive into the deeper and more soulful topics that impact your connection to yourself.

First, you'll explore confidence and how you can build it using acts of everyday courage. You'll learn about the surprising connection between confidence and personality. You'll meet people who have had great success building their confidence and you'll read some deeply honest social media posts about how to reconnect with the most important person in your life—yourself.

Second, you'll learn how everyday courage helps you discover your passion. You'll meet men and women who are using the #5SecondRule to win the battle with fear and find the courage to pursue what's in their hearts. Their examples will inspire you to do the same.

Third, you'll explore what creates deep and meaningful connections in relationships and why courage is such a critical component. The amazing stories in this section will inspire you to make the most of the time you have with the people you love and give you one simple thing that you can do at any moment and at any time to deepen your relationships.

Bring tissues.

This is my favorite section of the book. If you can enrich your self-confidence, passion, and connection with people, your life will transform in ways that you thought you could only dream of.

There will always be someone who can't see your worth.

Don't let it be you.

CHAPTER FIFTEEN

BUILDING REAL CONFIDENCE

"THE CAVE YOU FEAR TO ENTER HOLDS

THE TREASURE YOU SEEK."

JOSEPH CAMPBELL

A big mistake people make is thinking that confidence is a matter of personality. Confidence just means that you believe in yourself, your ideas, and your capabilities. Anyone can learn how to become more confident. It's not a personality trait. It's a skill.

You may have an extroverted personality and talk a lot, but that doesn't mean you are confident. The most vocal person in the room might be really insecure and only says what he thinks will make him look good. Look no further than me. For a long time, I was loud and bossy, but I felt insecure in myself, my ideas, and my abilities.

The quietest people you know might actually be the most confident. Your best friend who's an introvert might believe in her ideas with great confidence (and get annoyed when you don't ask her about them), but she's afraid of speaking up because her face turns red. She isn't lacking confidence in her ideas; she just needs a little courage to push through her fear of being judged for having rosy cheeks.

I had an experience that illustrates the connection between confidence, courage, and personality. It also will show you once again the authentic pride you feel when you 5- 4- 3- 2- 1 to push yourself outside your comfort zone.

Recently, I had a chance to speak at Cisco Systems, the largest networking technology and services company in the world. A few months later I was invited back to give a similar talk, this time to a senior engineering group.

When I arrived for that second talk, a man came up to me as I was setting up with the AV team. He was so excited to see me and greeted me with the warm embrace of an old friend. Being from the Midwest, I love nothing more than a good hug. He could hardly contain his excitement, and said that he "had something so exciting to tell me about the Rule."

He had seen me speak at Cisco Live several months back. During that speech, as I often do, I gave the audience a homework assignment using the #5SecondRule:

Introduce yourself to three strangers today, using the 5 Second Rule.

Then, I explained how I wanted them to do this assignment:

Pay attention to your instincts and the moment that you feel "drawn" toward someone. That's the "push moment." Grab it. Start counting 5- 4- 3- 2- 1 and start walking toward the person within five seconds before your mind talks you out of it.

Next, I explained to the audience what they can expect when they try this simple homework assignment. The moment that they see someone they'd like to meet their minds will fill up with a million excuses for why they shouldn't walk over and introduce themselves:

Oh…wait. They're talking to other people and I don't want to be rude; she looks busy so I'll catch her later; he's looking at his phone so I don't want to interrupt; there's not a lot of time so I'll do it at the next break.

And all of those things you think—they aren't true. Instead, it's your brain trying to derail you.

After my new engineer friend recapped my own assignment, he then described what had happened to him. After my speech, at Cisco Live, he was out in the hallway and he had a "push moment." John Chambers, Cisco's CEO, walked by with a group of senior leaders. Now, you must understand, John Chambers is a legend at Cisco and from all accounts, he's a really great guy. Chambers was the CEO for twenty years and the very next day, it was going to be announced that he would be stepping down as CEO and that Chuck Robbins would be taking over.

So, my new friend the engineer was standing in the hallway fresh from learning the #5SecondRule. He saw Chambers and his instincts fired up. He immediately had the urge to introduce himself and thank Chambers for inspiring him, along with letting him know the pride that he felt being an engineer at Cisco. He told me that he knew he should do it and he tried to push himself, but he froze.

He explained that he felt paralyzed, adding that he is an "introvert" and "this sort of thing" doesn't come naturally to him. The moment passed. His hero disappeared down the hall and he spent the remainder of the day beating himself up for not taking "his shot to meet him." But luckily, that's not the end of his story.

The next morning, my new friend was jogging next to the San Diego Bay in Embarcadero Park in downtown San Diego. This beautiful bike path along the Marina was (as usual) filled with runners, cyclists, and walkers. He had his earphones in and was listening to music, taking it all in. And all of a sudden, who do you think was ahead of him on the path? That's right, John Chambers.

Chambers was alone, he had his headphones on, and he's jogging too. My friend told me that he knew this was it. Now or never. He said, *"I was immediately concerned that I would be interrupting his time to himself and that it would be rude, but I caught myself hesitating and started counting down 5- 4- 3-..."*

He sped up to catch Chambers, tapped him on the shoulder, apologized for interrupting, and then explained how he had always wanted to personally thank him for the incredible career he has had at Cisco. The two men stopped jogging and started to walk through the Embarcadero together.

According to my friend, Chambers was delightful and engaging. They discussed all kinds of topics: work, life, and even an idea that my friend had related to a project he was working on. At the end of the talk, Chambers shook his hand, thanked him for introducing himself, and gave the engineer the name of a senior person in the organization in charge of innovation. "Use my name and tell him we spoke and that I wanted you to share your idea with him," Chambers said.

My new friend was beaming bright enough to light up the room as he told me the story. "It was the highlight of my career, Mel. And if it hadn't been for the #5SecondRule, it never would have happened. I cannot thank you enough."

And then he added, "Oh, my gosh, I almost forgot; I'm now interviewing for a job with the man Chambers introduced me to!"

Did he get the job?

I honestly have no idea. A new job isn't the point of the story. This is a story about acts of everyday courage and how they build confidence. This singular experience has the potential to change more than a job. If he continues to use the Rule to listen to and follow his instincts, it could very well change the trajectory of what's possible for his life.

His exuberance was not necessarily about meeting the CEO, although that's cool, but more about how darn good it feels when you honor your own desires and take control of your life.

Remember, confidence in yourself is built through acts of everyday courage. That's what he was experiencing: the radiance of knowing that he could count on himself. The more that my engineer friend practices acts of everyday courage, the more confident he'll become in himself.

Remember, confidence is created by the small things you do every single day that build trust in yourself.

I received a message from a man named Bill that will help me illustrate this point about learning to trust yourself. Bill described a struggle that so many of us face with a level of bravery that is inspiring.

"I Have An Issue Being the Real Me."

Bill's life on the outside sounds remarkable. He's married, has four great kids, a very successful career, and is the president of a professional association. "Great life, huh?" Sure sounds like it. But there's something missing. And it's a meaningful connection with himself.

Bill is courageous enough to admit that he's "not living with conviction" and that (like so many of us) he has developed a habit of "hesitating, overthinking, then never doing or saying what I should be doing or saying." Bill feels as though he's "lost somehow the ability to make a real connection with people."

He's forgetting the most important person he's lost connection with—himself. When you lose touch with the real you, you will feel adrift, you'll lose confidence and your life will lose its "flavor of congruency."

Bill

Thanks and kudos to you for having the guts to tell it like you see it. I am 53, a father of 4, with 3 grown up daughters and now a five year old kinder boy with my second wife. I am a Sr. Project Manager for my company as well as the manager of our Construction department. I also volunteer with the local PMI chapter, just getting into my President's terms. So, great life huh? Except I have an issue being the real me. I have lost somehow the ability to make a real connection with people. Things are not very exciting in the bedroom. I struggle with knowing what I really want. And I have a habit of hesitating, overthinking, then never doing or saying what I should be doing or saying. Nothing earth shattering, but just not living with conviction. My life just doesn't have that flavor of congruency. So, the five second rule come into my life the last Saturday at PMI NA LIM.

You can get it back with the #5SecondRule. Bill started using it to work on his relationship with himself. To go deep and "little by little" start walking the "journey of a thousand steps," pushing himself to do the small things that "quietly" teach you to trust yourself.

And little by little I have started the journey of a thousand steps. Getting up in the morning and walking the dogs. Being honest but tactful with people. Giving back every chance I get. Making tough decisions at work. Focusing on priorities and being able to say no when I need to. Getting out of bed and taking the dogs out. Just little steps but it is exhilarating exciting and also I am quietly learning to trust myself. A big difference because I am moving forward.

A good life is made up of small steps—"making tough decisions," "being able to say no," even "getting out of bed and taking the dogs out" just because you said you would—they may be little steps in "learning to trust" yourself, but they are the most "exhilarating" moves that you can make for your confidence.

Trayce is a 48-year-old stay-at-home mom who felt stuck in a rut when she discovered the #5SecondRule and "WHAM…like a light had been turned on." She uses the Rule to do things that "are small in the big scheme of things, but the feeling and uplift they give me is huge"—like speaking at church or posting a photo of herself online.

Here's the thing we learned from Bill: Small things are not small at all. They are the most important things of all. And they add up. Pushing yourself to 5- 4- 3- 2- 1 on the "small things" gives you confidence to do the "big scheme of things."

"Most of the applications were small in the big scheme of things, but the feeling and uplift they gave me is huge.

*Here is a brief list of some things I have done using the 5-second rule **that I would not have otherwise done**.*

I stood up and danced by myself at a music concert, I took and posted a picture of myself with an author I admire [I don't like pictures of myself], I spoke in front of a congregation in my church, I spoke to my husband about something that was bothering me, I introduced myself to people I wanted to meet, and I have accomplished more around my home [not putting things off as much].

In and of themselves, these are not earth shattering events, but I did them because of the power behind Mel's 5-second rule.

I am trying to use this tool now for things I consider to be bigger struggles such as losing extra weight I have been carrying around for 25 years and to getting up the courage to attend my 30-year High School Reunion, considering the amount of weight I have gained.

I even used the 5-second rule to write and submit my story. I also try to share Mel's message of the 5-second rule with others and have heard and seen some people putting it into practice for themselves. I know I will continue to use this empowering and yet so simple life-changing formula.

For the first time in a long time I feel like I am beginning to get unstuck and climb out of my rut…and I can't wait to see what happens next.

Thank you, Trayce"

Confidence builds when you do things that affirm your sense of self, particularly when they are things that you might not normally do, like getting up on time, speaking in front of your church, or chasing down the CEO of Cisco on a bike path. These are acts of everyday courage and they build confidence.

Crystal attended that same Cisco Live 2015 event as the engineer and she wrote to me about the #5SecondRule. She "realized that for the past 8 years" she had "second guessed every step" she had taken: *I thought someone was interesting and then a second later my mind would give me a million reasons why not to try to speak to them.*

She started implementing 5- 4- 3- 2- 1 and "right away" by first sitting next to people she didn't know in a break out session. The next day, when the instructor asked if anyone had any questions, she "realized I did but was embarrassed to even ask...then thought you know what you would have stood up if you just stopped thinking about it so I did."

Using the #5SecondRule, she stood up and asked her question. She also inspired two other women to stand up too in a room full of male engineers. Next, she 5- 4- 3- 2- 1 and made herself go to a basketball game when she didn't feel like it and even found the courage to ask a VP for a business card. Because of these acts of everyday courage her confidence has grown since the event and her life has completely changed: a new job, a new title, and a new house.

I attended Cisco Live 2015 and heard you talk about the 5 second rule. It was superb! I hadn't realized that for the past 8 years I had second guessed every step I had taken. I thought someone was interesting and then a second later my mind would give me a million reasons why not to try to speak to them. After having heard about your 5 second rule I found myself implementing it right away! I met people I wouldn't have met had I not.

I walked into a class full of people and searched for people I knew to sit next to them and then said hey what are you doing. Get your butt over there and meet new people sit anywhere. I did. Then when the instructor asked if anyone had any questions I realized I did but was embarrassed to even ask especially if I had to stand up. I then thought u know what you would have stood up if you just stopped thinking about it so I did. I stood up and asked my question.
After I did the other two girls in a room full of men did too.

It felt great! Later I was invited to watch a basketball game and at first it sounded great but then I thought I should rest at the hotel. I'm so glad I decided to go with my first instinct. I met the Cisco VP and even obtained their card!

The day I heard you at Cisco Live has changed a lot about me! I have a new job that pays me the amount I deserve. I have a new title (I jumped up three positions!). I finally took the leap to buy a house after many years of thinking about it. The least I can say is thank you. Thank you for opening my eyes to the 5 second rule which has made all the difference!

Nobuo started using the #5SecondRule after he was "released from an executive director" role. He lost his motivation and "felt incapable."

 Nobuo Kishi 2 years ago I happened to watch TEDX presentation of Mel Robbins. Listening to the Mel's talk I became to realize that the 5 second rule might be able to work for myself. After I was released from an executive director of a company, my life was changed completely not only mentally but also financially. I lost my motivation to create a new life and felt like I am incapable. However, the 5 second rule helped me a lot and I decided to apply the rule in to my daily life. After started using the rule, little by little the power and energy has come back to my heart, mind and body. I often quote Mel's comment on my blog and translate into Japanese.
Mel, pray for your success from the land of the rising sun.

Using the Rule to practice acts of everyday courage "little by little," Nobuo has found just like Crystal did that "the power and energy has come back to my heart, mind and body." It's come back because he has proven to himself that he has the power to change things in his life.

There's one more point I want to make about personality and confidence. Remember what the engineer said right after he described how he froze the first time he saw Chambers walk by in the hallway? He offered an explanation of sorts, "I'm an 'introvert' and 'this sort of thing' doesn't come naturally."

What if I told you that nothing about your life or personality is fixed or "comes naturally" anyway? Nothing comes naturally until you practice it. That's why I keep saying you must "practice" acts of everyday courage.

You have the ability to improve, change or enrich every single aspect of your life—through action. Professor Brian Little, a psychologist at the University of Cambridge, just gave a great TED Talk, *Who Are You, Really? The Puzzle of Personality.* In it, he talks about the difference between extroverts and introverts and the things that make us who we are. According to Professor Little, "It's the doings.

It's the personal projects." He describes how some of our traits are more fixed and automatic, but many are "free traits" that we can adjust in order to advance a core project in our lives.

Little explains that like the engineer at Cisco, he's also an introvert. However, his core, personal project is to profess. He loves to teach. So even as an introvert, he is "acting out of character" when he is up in front of the class connecting with his students. How does he do it? Through deliberate and purposeful action. He pushes himself to do it.

The engineer's personal project was to express his gratitude to John Chambers. That's why he had the instinct to "act out of character." How did he actually push himself to do it? The #5SecondRule. In both examples two things were present—a desire to do something meaningful (connect with students or a CEO) and deliberate action (a push to act out of character).

Does it feel harder for an introvert to walk up to a CEO, talk in front of her church, or teach a class than it feels for an extrovert to do these things? Maybe. Maybe not. Depends on how confident the individual is. And confidence, as you know, has nothing to do with personality.

As Professor Little likes to say, "you are like some other people and like no other person." What I do know is that the first time you do anything, it's going to feel difficult and maybe a little scary. You're going to need a little courage. We are all capable of "acting out of character" when it serves an important purpose. The most important purpose I can think of is improving your life in ways that make you come alive and feel happy and fulfilled.

How do you "act out of character" to do that work? You guessed it: you assert yourself and practice acts of everyday courage using the #5SecondRule. Those acts may not seem "earth shattering," but they will shatter self-doubt over time.

There's so much greatness inside each and every single one of us. The Rule helps us see how "freaking incredible" we all are, just as Amber discovered about herself.

> __amberoh__ @melrobbinslive you are freaking incredible and because of you, I now know so am I. You have inspired me!!!!! I reaaaaaaalllllllyyyy loved listening to you!

Which takes us back to the very beginning point: The more that you practice acts of courage, the more that you will believe you are in control of your life, and as a result, the more confident that you will become. Even when what you need to do scares you to death, the Rule helps you take courageous action. Michelle found the courage to quit her "toxic, anxiety ridden job" and even though she's "scared of the unknown," that one act of everyday courage has made her "more confident in myself and capabilities."

I quit my toxic, anxiety ridden job this week, and while I am SO scared of the unknown coming up, I've never felt more confident in myself and capabilities after reading Stop Saying Your Fine. I want to thank you so deeply for pushing me to go for something better. You're changing me without even knowing it! You rock!

As Michelle discovered, doing things that scare you actually make you more confident. If you have the courage to take action, your confidence will follow. Every time you push yourself to speak when you're nervous, act when you're afraid, or get to the gym when you don't feel like it, you realize that you can rely on yourself to get anything done. From this belief in your personal abilities flows your confidence.

Jay goes to a performing arts high school in Toronto but has "always been nervous to go out for things." Using the Rule, he has auditioned for more roles, gotten more parts in shows, and he's also "gained a lot of self-confidence."

The more that you use the Rule, the faster your confidence will grow. Stacey uses the Rule "almost daily" to act with courage and "talk to people face to face," "do home shows" for her business, and "no longer hide" because of fear. Using the Rule in acts of everyday courage has helped her "grow in ways I never thought possible." She has cultivated the confidence she's always wanted and it feels "amazing."

Throughout this book, you have read stories of people who have taken very simple or seemingly small steps forward—and their entire outlook on life has changed. It's tempting to dismiss these stories because it seems implausible that by simply waking up on time every morning, you can create a chain reaction that impacts your confidence. However, this is exactly how you do it. Stop focusing on the big things. Use 5- 4- 3- 2- 1-GO on the smallest things—and you will see that these moments are actually not so small.

As Bill said, daily courageous actions of getting out of bed, making tough decisions, being able to say no, giving back every chance you get, and focusing on priorities create a ripple effect that change your life. These are little steps but the payoff is everything that you seek: confidence, control, and a sense of pride that feels damn good.

**Speak
from your
heart,
even if
your
voice
shakes.**

CHAPTER SIXTEEN

PURSUING PASSION

> "THERE'S A VOICE THAT DOESN'T
>
> USE WORDS, LISTEN."
>
> RUMI

Over the years, I've received lots of questions about how to find your passion and purpose. Not once have I ever been asked to help someone *"think about their passion."* That's because finding your passion is an active process and you'll find that the #5SecondRule is an incredible tool as opportunities start to appear. What stops people from finding their passion is that can't get out of their thoughts and move into action. When you use the #5SecondRule to 5- 4- 3- 2- 1 push yourself to start exploring and lean into opportunities as they appear, you'll be shocked where it leads.

Start Exploring

How do you explore? Hire the best guide you can find: your curiosity. Your curiosity is how your instincts get you to pay attention to what your heart really cares about. If you can't stop thinking something, make something your new hobby. Also pay close attention to envy. If you find yourself jealous of someone else, explore that feeling. What aspect of their life are you jealous of? This may give you a clue into what you really want for yourself.

Next, push yourself to take simple steps to explore that subject: read about it, watch video tutorials, talk to people, take a class, and write a plan. You'll be surprised by what happens over time.

Your passion could be photography. When Chris first discovered the #5SecondRule four years ago, he was a CIO at a bank (and he still is), and he had always loved photography. He used the Rule to force himself to explore his passion, and, two magazine covers and multiple awards later, he's a professional photographer.

 **Chris Auditore**

Mel Robbins
So Friday prior to the Stagger Moon Band shoot at Sewannee I received an email from an amazing woman named Mel Robbins. Mel's principles of the 5 second rule has led me down the path of 4 covers, Multiple awards and voted Finest Photographer just to name a few things. Her principle is simple. If you have an idea act on it in the first 5 seconds. Simple right? Not so for a lot of us. Ideas pop into our creative heads all the time and we just let them drift away. So after watching her TED talk about 4 years ago I was convinced I could do this! Well ladies and gentleman I am here to tell you that creatively it is amazing. When an idea pops into your head either write it down or just do it ! It really is simple.

Maybe you're interested in launching a gourmet food business. It doesn't matter if you've never done it before. In today's world, you have so many resources at your disposal to help you explore. Take Eric as an example. He lives in Cambodia and had an idea to start an export business. He's pushing himself to learn everything he can by watching YouTube videos and reading books.

 Eric

I currently live in Cambodia and have been here almost two years. I came here after a divorce to teach English, as well as, to learn to be content being by myself.

Lately I've felt very homesick yet my gut had told me that if I returned to Atlanta, GA (where I'm from) I would regret it.

I've had an idea of wanting to start a business exporting some rare food items from here that are not available in the US and should be as I want to share these wonderful ingredients from this lovely country w/ people in the US. I have a great friend in Atlanta that runs a gourmet food wholesale distribution company that sells many comparable niche items.

I have a product, I have a way to distribute the product, yet I had no idea how to start yet run my own business. Since I watched your TED talk I have purchased and already read half of a 'starting your own import/export business' book along w/ several YouTube videos.

 For the first time in my life, I have an idea that I'm passionate about that could actually become my own business.

That's how you "discover" your passion, you 5- 4- 3- 2- 1 explore until you bump into it.

Build Momentum

It will start as just an instinct. It always does. First you take a class. A class leads to a certification. A certification leads to conversations. Conversations lead to opportunities. Small opportunities lead to larger ones. Maybe you'll want to share something what you're learning with people at work, so you use the Rule push yourself to do it. That's when momentum kicks in.

You'll curse me as things actually start to happen, but you'll thank yourself for finding the courage to trust your heart and explore what you find fascinating. Jo, a banker in London, is a fabulous example of how something small, like taking one class, can grow into something remarkable like a whole new career. This story is an unbelievable example of how momentum builds from something small. Check this out:

Jo, a banker in London, is a fabulous example of how something small, like taking one class, can grow into something remarkable like a whole new career. This story is an unbelievable example of how momentum builds from something small. Check this out:

Joanne McLellan
View Profile

I did a presentation on limiting beliefs and an introduction to our 'maps of the world' at my team meeting of 8 people - I was nervous but I did it as I'd recently qualified as a master NLP Practitioner and I wanted to share what I'd learnt. When the presentation ended my head of function walked up to me and said "this is what you should be doing, you could make a career doing this" (I currently work in banking, I'm.....a banker). To say I was buzzing after this and the other feedback I got made me feel awesome was an understatement. I got brave and decided to put the 5 second rule In action so I went to my laptop and typed an email to one of the largest women's network in the UK (managed by Lloyds Banking Group, my bank) called Breakthrough to offer my services. I think I actually posted on your Facebook page that morning something like "5 second rule in action today"! Long story short they came back and said they would love me to do presentation to their Scotland

devision. Fast forward a couple weeks to Tuesday last week and a very nervous me was, I'll be honest, cursing you and the 5 second rule as I was terrified but I did the presentation and you know what?!? I was so good we have a waiting list of people who couldn't make it (due to the line being blocked out, timing of the first session and word of mouth on how good it was) so I've been asked to run a second session! I've also been approached about jobs and people are asking me to help them work through their limiting beliefs and supper them with their goals (or outcomes)! All of this happened because of the 5 second rule and sending one email! Oh I should also mention I gave Stop Saying your fine a shout out as one my favourite books at the end of the presentation as people asked for books that have inspired me 😊

This stuff works and I tell at everyone to give it a go and see where it gets them - maybe even where they want to be 😊

Jo
Banker and Coach (I guess)

As your exploration picks up momentum, you'll move into the next phase— actually pursuing your passion full-time. At some point, the side business of photography will become your real business. Your presentation to the Bank of Scotland will become a full-blown speaking career.

The Courage to Commit

There's no magic formula for when to pull the trigger and turn a passion project into a passion-driven career or major life change. It requires planning and some slow, deep thinking. If you are anything like the rest of us, you'll torture yourself for a while until you can't stand straddling your present life and the future one.

Michal had a major passion that she wanted to turn into a company and had "been wanting to do it for years but have just held back." She 5- 4- 3- 2- 1 pushed herself "to announce the start of my new business." Now, she has a reason to "not hit that snooze button" anymore.

 Michal Lowthorpe I used the 5 second rule today to announce the start of my new business of horse & rider portraits. I have been wanting to do it for years but have just held back. I can't wait and now have something to not hit that snooze button for! Thank you Mel

We all deserve to wake up so excited that we no longer want to "hit that snooze button," just like Michal. If you are thinking about making the leap like her, make sure to be intentional about how you ask yourself the question.

You need to ask yourself the Heart First question, *"Am I ready to commit to this?"* instead of the Feeling First question, *"Do I feel ready to commit to this?"* You'll never *feel* ready. The moment you answer yes to the question *"Am I ready to commit to this?"* you'll need to use the Rule to give yourself that final push.

Even when you are ready, it's not going to *feel* good when you do it. Just ask Todd in Australia. Todd has known for a long time exactly what he is passionate about: physical education. He's always dreamed of teaching it and having his own personal training business. As a high-schooler, Todd knew that he wanted pursue a degree in Physical Education, but his parents said, *"Oh no, you can't do that…"* They pressured him to pursue a "professional" degree instead.

Four years later, Todd was a senior in a dual major program split between Law and Business. His heart was never in it. As Todd described in an email, that "little voice" was constantly in the back of his head "silently" echoing. Why did he stay in that major? Simple—his feelings. The thought of disappointing his parents overwhelmed him. Every single day, he thought about withdrawing and going to a different college to study Physical Education, but he felt paralyzed. Walking into the Registrar's Office and filling out paperwork is easy. Facing the disappointment of your parents is soul-crushing.

For almost four years, Todd had wanted to withdraw, but he didn't know *how* to face his fears or his parents. The #5SecondRule is how he finally did it. Todd was sitting in a LAWS5513 Lecture on Advanced Taxation Law when he realized that he was "ready."

As Todd put it:

"I can attest to you the dislike I had for such a program; I wanted to withdraw from the moment I started. But what is perhaps, most disturbing about this entire situation is that I had literally allowed myself to study a degree up to the final year before I decided I was entirely and completely done with hating my life!"

Todd could see the future:

"My parents would send me off to do my Masters and along I would go, living my life…for everyone, but me!"

He described the instinct to act and the five second decision that made it happen.

"Just start. I need to withdraw. I gathered up my books and stood up in the middle of class and left."

His body was shaking, but he was moving—straight to the Registrar's Office, where he unenrolled from the University. He then got in the car and drove two hours south of Brisbane to The Queensland University of Technology, where he applied for the degree of his dreams.

That fateful Tuesday morning was two years ago. Todd is now 24 years old and halfway through his teaching degree and has "never had this much fun in my life." He has been accepted into the honors Education program for next year. As he puts it:

"I have found my purpose ... this is in fact exactly what I was supposed to be doing all along."

As for his parents, yes they were disappointed when he initially told them that he didn't want to be a lawyer, but they were way more disappointed by the fact that Todd had been scared (to tell them) and unhappy for so long.

Have Faith

I believe you can make anything happen as long as you listen to your heart, do the work, and give up your timeline. One of my favorite books is the international best-seller *The Alchemist*. It's one of the best-selling books of all time and has been translated into 80 languages. I've recommended it for more than a decade, and as I was writing this book, I bought myself a new copy to keep me inspired and reminded that the *"Whole universe conspires to help you when you follow your heart."*

When I cracked open the twenty-fifth anniversary edition, I was blown away by a story in the forward of the book. I had no idea that when *The Alchemist* was first published in Brazil, it failed. Miserably.

"When The Alchemist *was first published twenty-five years ago in my native Brazil, no one noticed. A bookseller in the northeast corner of the country told me that only one person purchased a copy the first week of its release. It took another six months for the bookseller to unload a second copy—and that was to the same person who bought the first! And who knows how long it took to sell the third.*

By the end of the year, it was clear to everyone that The Alchemist *wasn't working. My original publisher decided to cut me loose and cancelled our contract. They wiped their hands of the project and let me take the book with me. I was forty-one and desperate.*

But I never lost faith in the book or ever wavered in my vision. Why? Because it was me in there, all of me, heart and soul. I was living my own metaphor. A man sets out on a journey, dreaming of a beautiful or magical place, in pursuit of some unknown treasure. At the end of his journey, the man realizes the treasure was with him the entire time."

Forty-one and desperate? I got chills when I read that line. That's how old I was when I discovered the #5SecondRule, and that's exactly how I felt. What I have come to realize is there is no expiration date on discovering and expressing the power of you. And as Coelho wrote in the foreword, it starts with a belief in yourself, and that belief is grounded in the courage to push yourself.

"I was following my Personal Legend, and my treasure was my capacity to write. And I wanted to share this treasure with the world. I started knocking on the doors of other publishers. One opened, and the publisher on the other side believed in me and my book and agreed to give The Alchemist a second chance. Slowly, through word of mouth, it finally started to sell—three thousand, then six thousand, ten thousand—book by book, gradually throughout the year."

The book became an organic phenomenon and the rest is history. It is considered one of the ten best books of the twentieth century. When interviewers ask Coelho whether or not he knew that it would be a success, this is what he had to say:

"The answer is no. I had no idea. How could I? When I sat down to write The Alchemist, all I knew is that I wanted to write about my soul. I wanted to write about my quest to find my treasure."

The answers are inside of you if you have the courage to listen. You are like some other people and like no other person. You have something remarkable to share with the world. It starts with listening to what's inside of you and ends with the courage to go where it leads.

Follow it.

Don't tell people your dreams.
Show them.

CHAPTER SEVENTEEN

ENRICH YOUR RELATIONSHIPS

> **"AN ACT OF COURAGE IS ALWAYS**
>
> **AN ACT OF LOVE."**
>
> **PAULO COELHO**

There are only two words of advice you need to improve any relationship.

Say It

I was speaking at a sales meeting for a retail brokerage firm in Florida and afterward a tall man named Don approached me. He was in his late 50s, had a beard, and was wearing a sport coat over his madras shirt. He said he wanted to share something with me about "my 5 Second Rule."

Don had "his own version of it that had changed his life." He had "made a decision a few years ago, that nothing important would be left unsaid."

Then he shared a story about how, acting on instinct, he pushed himself to share something with his daughter that had completely changed their entire relationship. Over the years his daughter Amber and her husband had taken in family members who had fallen on hard times. They also volunteered every weekend in their community and had completed several service trips.

Don told them that he admired them. He admired how they lived their lives and the example that their lives provided the world. He added that he was so proud of the young woman Amber had become. And then he told me this: "Right before I was about to say it. I was so afraid. Imagine that. I was afraid to say something because I was afraid to get emotional."

He said that after that conversation, his relationship with his daughter was never the same again. They are now closer than he ever imagined and the experience inspired him to live by this rule: *Leave nothing important unsaid.*

Intimacy takes courage. Risking getting emotional or upsetting someone so that you can express yourself is scary, but the result is magical. I experienced that same magic in a simple conversation with my father last fall. I was on my way to the airport having just finished a speaking engagement in Miami and I saw a text from my dad: "Call me as soon as you can."

That's odd, I thought to myself. I called the house, and my mom picked up the phone.

"Hi Mom, I just got a text from Dad asking me to call. Is everything okay?"

"You should talk to him, let me get him for you…"

She set the phone down, as I tried to catch her

"Wait, Mom! What's going on?"

I could hear the kitchen door creak as she opened it and yelled for my dad, "BOB! Mel's on the phone!"

I had no idea what was going on. At first, I thought that I was in trouble. I sat in the back of that cab feeling like a 10-year-old who was about to get grounded.

Isn't it amazing how quickly your mind can take you down the rabbit hole that something is wrong?

Uncertainty had triggered my habit of worrying and now I was inside the mental "What-if Loop": *Did grandma die? Did I do something wrong? Is he in financial trouble? It must be me, what did I do?*

Did you catch what happened? The uncertainty triggered my habit of worrying. In less than five seconds, I had convinced myself that my grandmother had died, that I had done something severely wrong, that my father was deeply disappointed in me, or that I was about to get in major trouble.

I heard the back door open and him walking toward the kitchen. He picked up the phone and was as nonchalant as could be, *"Hey Mel, thanks for calling, where are you right now?"*

I was freaking out on the other end of the line.

"I'm in Miami on my way to the airport, your text scared me to death, did I do something wrong?"

He chuckled and said, *"No, it's not about you, Mel. It's about me. I didn't want to tell you and your brother until I was sure."*

I almost dropped the phone. *"Are you gonna die? Oh my god, you have cancer."*

He interrupted, *"Will you let me talk…I don't have cancer. I have an aneurism and I need open brain surgery to remove it before it kills me."*

He went on to explain the whole story. He had had a bout of vertigo and collapsed while he was playing a round of golf. That lead to an MRI, which revealed this aneurism. They found it by mistake. He was having surgery at the end of the week at the University of Michigan.

I sat frozen on the other side of the phone. My father-in-law had died from esophageal cancer. Within seconds of hearing my dad's story, I immediately thought about the day of my father-in-law's surgery. It was just a moment. The nurses were wheeling him off to surgery at Memorial Sloan Kettering in Manhattan and just before they pushed him through the double doors, he looked back at all of us.

He smiled and gave us a little wave. We all smiled and waved back, and I remember giving him a "thumbs up." I remember feeling a pang of fear right at that moment. Then he disappeared through the swinging doors. We had no idea that his surgery was about to go horribly wrong and that the complications would eventually kill him.

I snapped back into the present moment, in the back of the cab and listened to my dad. I pictured my father waving goodbye from a hospital hallway, and I was afraid. I don't know why, but I really wanted to know if my dad was scared too. I had an instinct to ask him and immediately hesitated. I started think.

"Don't ask that, it'll upset him. Of course he's scared, you moron. Keep it light and positive. Don't stress him out, that aneurysm could explode." That was the push moment. *Leave nothing important unsaid.*

5..4..3..2..1..

"Dad, are you scared?"

There was silence on the other end. And I started to regret asking the question. I was not expecting to hear what he said next:

"I'm not scared. I am nervous, but I really trust my surgeon. You know, Mel, I actually feel kind of lucky."

"Lucky?" That's not what I expected to hear.

"Yes, I have an opportunity to try and fix this thing before it kills me. And at the end of the day if something happens I have no regrets. Watching my mom take care of my dad after his

stroke or watching Susie die of ALS was horrible. Quality of life is very important to me. And the quality of my life has been more than I could have ever wished for. As a kid I always wanted to be a doctor, and I became one. Your mom and I have had a wonderful life together. You and your brother turned out. I've basically done exactly what I wanted to do with my life. And that's all you can ever ask for…that and more time to enjoy it."

It was one of the most beautiful moments I have ever shared with my dad and without the #5SecondRule, I wouldn't have found my courage to ask the question. I just sat there in the back of that cab and took it all in. And then he added this:

"Actually, there is one thing I want to do," he said, *"I'd like to see Africa. And if I make it to 90, I want to jump out of plane like George H. Bush did on his 90th birthday."*

I laughed. *"You will dad, you will."*

That conversation with my dad reminded me of something important. Waiting for the right time to get real in your relationships is a fool's errand. There is no right time to have the conversation, ask the hard questions, say "I love you," or take the time to truly listen. There is only right now.

Sometimes it's not merely a hard question that you need to ask. It's actually ending the silence between you. It had been "years since" Cortney let her relationship go with her father, but she had been wanting to make amends. She didn't "pass out or over think it," like she would have in the past. Instead, she used the #5SecondRule to trust her instinct and just pick up the phone and call her dad. She just "said out loud 5- 4- 3- 2- 1 and just hit call and did it."

It only takes five seconds to change your life.

Mel
I have to tell you I listened to you in Salt Lake City a month ago and came home on fire. I actually used it to make mens with my father. It had been years since I let things go and moved on and I actually sat in my fiancés room and said out loud 5-4-3-2-1 and just hit call and did it. And I didn't pass out or over think it like I used to. So thank you for not only helping in my business but also personally. And every morning I use it to get by butt out of bed and go for a run.
Thank you thank you thank you
Cortney

Hiding is what Mike was doing in his marriage, until he found the courage to 5-4- 3- 2- 1 to be "more honest with" himself:

"I am talking to my wife again about subjects I would have rather just been ignored (not like they were going away because my head was in the sand or anything). And I am being more honest with myself. And most of all I like that. I may not be perfect, but I am worthy. I'm surprised by just how damn good that feels – to be worthy."

—Mike

Mike just shared a very powerful secret. To feel worthy, you must first make your own instincts worthy of your attention and your effort. And Anthony was surprised that "something so simple" as having the courage to "lean into what I normally shy away from" could create such "enormous change" in his marriage, helping him to be "closer to my wife" and get his needs met.

"That something so simple could create such enormous change. That was surprising. I used to expect people to know my needs and would harbor resentment when my needs were not met, mostly with my wife. I thought all wives could read minds, imagine my surprise.

By using the Rule to simply lean into what I normally would shy away from I'm making great strides in a few areas of my life. I'm smiling as I type this. I'm closer to my wife and my needs are starting to be met. I had no idea that my silence was the problem."

—Anthony

As Anthony said he "had no idea that my silence was the problem." Silence is always the problem. Deciding not to say what you feel creates what researchers call "cognitive dissonance" between what you truly believe (in your heart) and what you actually do in the moment. Those problems build up and, over time, they can break your relationship.

That's what happened to Estelle during what she described as "an ordinary moment in time." A seemingly stupid argument with her husband "cracked a branch in a silent woods" and her response was immediate—"I asked him for a divorce." Here's how she described it:

"My mind was suddenly crystal clear and I used the #5SecondRule to say it. It was now my choice to do it, or allow my brain to "pull the emergency brake." I chose in that moment, to act. I asked for a divorce. In retrospect that decision catapulted my life in the direction I knew I wanted to go, but always held myself back from.

This is not to say it was easy. It absolutely has not been easy, but I have never for one second doubted my decision. In that pure moment of action, of truly choosing to act on what I knew was right and authentically me, I have found myself. There have been dark and sometimes lonely moments, but what surprises me is that in those moments I never regret my choice to divorce.

We all have moments throughout our day to act or to choose. We sometimes hold ourselves back, we choose to be cautious and not act and to not risk. I choose to act. And it is in these moments that I feel most alive, have found my soulmate and more importantly my true self."

—Estelle

I said from the beginning that the Rule was simple. I never said it "saying it" would be easy. The truth is the shortest distance between two people and it may very well save your relationship. Silence creates distance. Truth creates real connection, as Natasha discovered.

Natasha was "overwhelmed with life" after her mother died suddenly. Her optimism "evaporated" and she could "only see more negatives" in the future. She was worried about her relationship with her boyfriend and used the Rule to 5- 4- 3- 2- 1 to "speak from the heart" about how she felt, for real—that their relationship "was unsustainable." She spoke how she really felt and the outcome was amazing. Instead of blowing up the relationship, the truth brought them closer. They're now engaged.

First one is a small one really. I work 10 hour days and by Thursday I'm usually shattered. I use the 5 second rule to give me a boost to do chores when really I'd love to crash on the sofa! I get the impulse to empty the dishwasher. I count to 5, get up, do it and then its done!

My second one is a bit bigger & linked to your first book too. I was having a difficult time at the start of the year after my mother passed away suddenly from cancer. I found myself getting overwhelmed often with life in general. My usual optimism evaporated. My 3 year relationship was suffering as a result. I felt daily anxiety that something bad would happen and I was worried the relationship was unsustainable as I couldn't see any positives in the future only more negatives. In June 2016, after realising I was not fine, I used the 5 second rule to start a conversation about my relationship. I explained how I felt, and how I wanted things to be better but I didn't know how to fix it. My partner patiently listened to me, and we took time out to talk and connect. We ended up receiving help from a relationship counsellor to help us gain new perspectives. We realised how much we had been through, how resilient we were as a couple, and how I had nothing to fear about our connection being broken. We have been nurturing our relationship for the past 2 months and I now live without fear. I am confident in our connection! This was reinforced more at the weekend when my boyfriend proposed! Of course I said yes, and I am the happiest I have ever been! 😊 I had no idea what the outcome of my original conversation would be. But I knew I needed to speak from the heart and see what happened. The outcome has been amazing! And I'm so grateful I didn't let fear paralyze me.

Thanks for reading!

We often fail to appreciate the profound power held inside the smallest moments of our relationships as our days race by. I recently had something happen that reminded me of the importance of slowing down, being present, "saying it," and tuning into your heart when it speaks to you.

A man sent me a Facebook message after hearing me speak, and asked me to check out a memorial page for a family friend named Josh Woodruff. He felt that Josh was the epitome of a person who lived his life to the fullest, and embodied the #5SecondRule.

On an instinct, I clicked on the link to the memorial page on Facebook. The first thing I saw was a post from a woman named Mary. It was a beautiful post about the intimacy and connectedness we all want in life and how we pull back from it for the silliest reasons. A week before Josh was killed by a hit-and-run driver in New Orleans, Mary had seen him in the grocery store but "didn't say anything to him." I'll let her tell you the story:

Mary Tacy Bazis
22 hrs · Omaha, NE

Josh and my son Jared have been friends since 2nd grade. We consider the Woodruffs some of our dearest and most admired friends.

The week before Josh died, I saw him twice in the grocery store. The first time, he was quite aways away and I thought "Oh there's Josh, he must be home for Christmas" but I didn't say anything to him because I didn't want to holler across the store. The same week I saw him again, with a big grin and stocking cap on talking to someone. He was much closer and I still didn't say anything because I had run to the store, quick, with no makeup and dressed horrid , just hoping I didn't see anyone i knew. I thought "Odd that i would see him twice in one week", so i prayed for his family and their Christmas holiday.

When I heard he died, I felt so bad I hadn't talked to him. i didn't know that would be the last time. But my last image of him was that huge, light up the world smile.

Last week, I was in Target and I saw a friend, Jenny, quite aways away. I started to walk out the door when I remembered Josh. I was in a hurry and didn't see any reason stop and talk, then I thought again of Josh. I turned around, and hollered down the aisle "Hey Jenny!..."

Mary's post is an incredible reminder for all of us. Sometimes there is no next time. When your heart speaks—say it. I reached out to Josh's mom, Caren, and she shared a story about Josh with me:

"Josh was not afraid of other people's emotions. When he was a teenager, my mother was diagnosed with cancer. I knew we were losing her. One day, I sat in the family room by myself to think and to cry. Josh came in and asked me what was wrong, and then "eye locked" me. He didn't look away or fidget. He just sat there and listened. From that day we started moving from just a mother-son to a friend-friend relationship because he took the time to listen to me as a human being."

I'm sad that I never got the chance to meet Josh. He sounded like an amazing man. As Caren described him, *"Josh was the epitome of doing. He took his intentions and acted on them. After his death, we said that he lived life without hesitation."*

She closed her email to me by attaching a text that Josh had sent to her and her husband on New Year's Eve, just hours before he was killed. As Caren put it, *"He thought it, he sent it. We will treasure it for the rest of our lives."*

To: Mark, Josh

Thursday 5:10 PM

Josh

Before the night begins, just wanted to say Happy New Year and that I'm so ridiculously thankful for ya! Very much pumped to see what 2016 has for us!

Thursday 6:42 PM

Happy new year !! We are SO thankful for you, and for the life you bring to us and to our family. Stay safe tonight. (I had to say that. I'm the mom :-))

📷 Text Message Send

Leave nothing important unsaid.

5- 4- 3- 2- 1 go ahead and say it.

All our dreams can come true if we have the courage to pursue them.

- Walt Disney

THE POWER OF YOU

> "YOU'VE ALWAYS HAD THE POWER MY DEAR,
>
> YOU JUST HAD TO LEARN IT FOR YOURSELF."
>
> GLINDA, THE WIZARD OF OZ

Today, something incredible is going to happen.

A woman will quit her job because she truly hates it. She is scared, but she'll do it anyway. A man will call off his wedding, knowing he'll be hated for it. A 56-year-old veterinarian will start her first business, an app developer will launch her first product, and a 15-year-old will start writing his first cookbook.

A banker will apply for an executive role that she's always wanted. She doesn't feel 100% qualified but that's not going to stop her from throwing her hat in the ring. And a man in a bar will leave the safety of his friends to walk across the room to approach an attractive woman. Initially, he'll feel like he's dying inside, but it will turn out way better than he anticipated.

They know they might fail or fall flat on their faces, but they do it anyway. They push themselves forward despite the feelings that scream "NO!" They feel afraid but they still move.

The question is, why? The answer is simple: they know the secret to greatness. When your heart speaks, honor it, 5- 4- 3- 2- 1- and move. They also know the alternative and that it is terrifying: missing out on all that you are meant to become. Living on autopilot and swimming right past all the magic, opportunity, and joy that your life has to offer. And the greatest risk of all? Dying before you've actually pushed yourself to live.

Dan in California is not going to let that happen. He's just registered for summer classes in finance. The idea of being a #44yearoldfreshman is daunting, but he does it anyway, because "never too old" is what it means to be great.

Dan Francis
@RealDanFrancis

@melrobbins damn your #5SecondRule I'm now registered for summer classes.
#44yearoldfreshman #nevertooold #business #finance

In Honolulu, Shirley is pushing herself to start living again after losing her husband. She's let too many "five second windows be wasted" over the last four years. Now, she is practicing everyday courage. She has started with something small —beginning to walk again. That one change has opened doors that have been closed for years.

Just want to let you know you inspired me to start walking again. This is a park at the end of Waikiki. Thank you, Mel. Aloha.

In Santa Monica, California, Julie used the #5SecondRule to push herself to make calls that made her nervous, and got two things: greater confidence in herself and $5,000 to help cure pancreatic cancer.

Julie Weiss
@MarathonGoddess

@melrobbins ThankYou This Donation to fight #pancreaticcancer happened because of the #5secondrule.

In New Delhi, India, Pulkit is taking "so many risks" using the #5SecondRule that it is helping him grow in "amazing" ways. He's now always "giving the best shot" at what he does, thanks to the Rule. And he has a piece of advice for Dan, our 44-year-old freshman: keep pushing. Pulkit knows the power of everyday courage because he just finished his bachelor's degree.

Pulkit

Hi Mel! :) Your 5 Second Rule really helped me a lot in my personal and professional life. From taking those little risks, from inculcating that, the execution, the effect is just amazing. I used to be an introvert, now I've striked a balance well. Yes, I love to talk :) I wouldn't have been able to achieve that without the 5 second rule. I've taken so many risks with my life and it just helps me grow using the 5 second rule, always giving the best shot at it. It has just turned out amazing :) I just completed my bachelors.

After a high stress week at work, Kathleen wanted to just "kick back and feel the buzz of a well-deserved drink and not deal" but she 5- 4- 3- 2- 1 and drove past the familiar cars at the bar. It was a "white knuckle" drive home, but in that moment she won. As Kathleen put it "However small that drive was, it felt like a victory." And it truly was.

KATHLEEN
to me

Dear Mrs. Robbins;

This Friday while driving home, all I could think about was the five second rule and the idea that you have to 'push' your way through certain situations to get unstuck. I have a significant commute so I got some good thinking time in. The industry I work in is very high stress, very deadline oriented my hours are oddball, I am out of work by two in the afternoon. So on this Friday, before a holiday, I would usually go meet friends at a local pub, have a few drinks and bitch and moan about the week. Lately I've felt as though the weekly bitch session has become nothing but an excuse for a brain numb, I felt as though I was avoiding my life and hiding behind Bombay Sapphire (although delicious and the nectar of the Gods is not a good place to play hide and seek). While getting off the exit that would bring me to the pub I started laughing, 'so this is what it means to push through, and NO, I do not feel like it.' I realized what you said was 100% on. No, I did not feel like going home, looking at my finances, dealing with my who cares attitude about how I live, I wanted to kick back feel the buzz of a well deserved drink and not deal...but I did, I saw all of the familiar cars in the parking lot and I drove by, trust me I white knuckled that drive.

However small that drive by was, it felt like a victory. I came home and turned on my laptop, looked at my finances, made a map. Like you, I'm a runner, I was training for an ultramarathon when I was injured, the dreaded achilles, I quit exercising period, I hate the gym... HATE IT, but have decided to go back a little at a time (I still hate it). After deciding to get my act together I asked fellow runners in a local forum for help finding a DR. After seeing this specialist she told me the issue with my achilles is 'fixable' and I should be out racing again by spring 2017.

This email was also part of the 5 second rule, I don't know if you'll ever see it, but I wrote it and sent it.

Have an excellent holiday weekend

In Minnesota, Kelly has made a Heart First five-second decision after years of dreaming about it. She's moving to France. Now that she's decided, the fear has disappeared just like Rosa Parks said it would, and she'll use her brain to figure out the details instead of allowing fear to hold her back.

Mel –
Thanks for sharing
My 5 seconds... I'm
now moving to
France.   Kelly

In London, England, Steve was suffering from PTSD and thinking about ending his life as he rode on a ferry. His instincts told him to get help and the #5SecondRule "kicked in," he moved away from the railing, and walked toward a steward working on the ferry. It took the lowest moment of his life to admit just how lost in depression he had become, but in less than five seconds he 5- 4- 3- 2- 1 and discovered the courage to save his life.

 **Steve**

@melrobbins you saved my life today, I was on the point of committing suicide. Was going to jump off a ferry. 5 sec R kicked in Thanks

 **Mel Robbins**
@melrobbins

Steve @montgomerysms what can we do to help you get help. Email hello@melrobbins.com we r here for u

 **Steve**

@melrobbins Now getting help xx

And finally, James…

Steve's story hit James "close to my heart." James lost his baby brother to suicide just a year ago. As James wrote, "I wish my brother took 5. I can never change that, but I can change myself." Using the #5SecondRule, he has found the courage he needs to wake up and start living again: "It's time for me to move on, back to my passion, back to my running." James made a five second decision. He is running a 100 miler, 5- 4- 3- 2- 1, in memory of his brother Patrick.

 **James**

Thank you so much. This was the highlight of conference for me. Prior to losing my baby brother to suicide on 6/8/15 I had run 18- 1/2 marathons and two full. After he passed, I couldn't run anymore. Running was my escape, time to reflect and think. I didn't want to do any of them anymore.

You spoke of the solider who was ready to jump off the bridge but did 5.4.3.2.1 and moved on. That hit me, close to my heart. I wish my brother took 5. I can never change that, but I can change myself.

It is time for me to move on, back to my passion, back to my running. I have been fighting with myself to run a 100 miler in memory of my brother but couldn't get the "push" I needed to make it reality.

Today I am taking 5.4.3.2.1 in memory of Patrick Stripling.

Thank you so much! I will be passing this along.

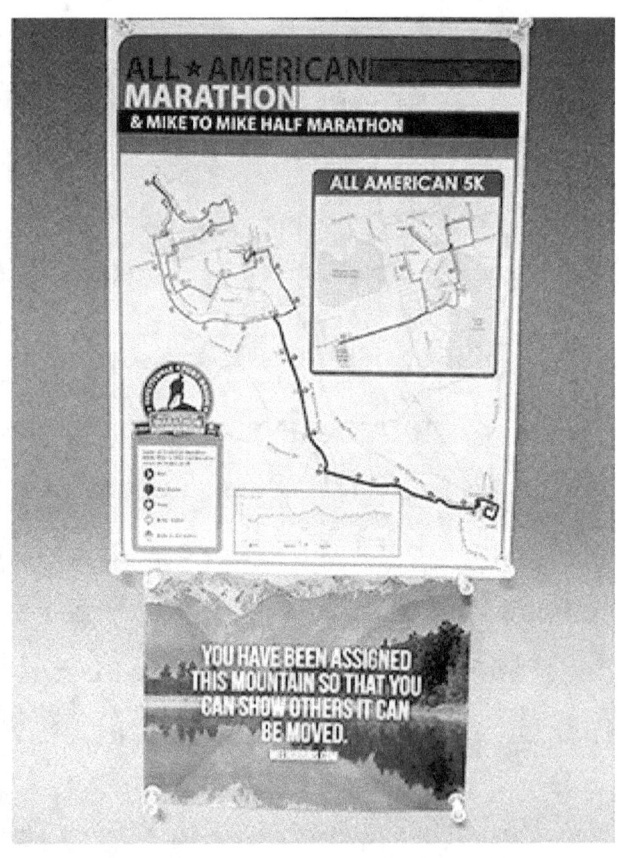

 **James**

Perfect Quote for my comeback. Right next to my desk so I will see it everyday and be reminded that I can move the mountain that stands before me.

#4Patrick #StopSuicide #BeTheVoice #YouAreEnough

Yes, you can move mountains. Whatever is happening right now, this is it. This is your life. And it's not going to begin again. You can't change the past, but in five seconds you can change your future.

That's the power of everyday courage. When your heart speaks, honor it, 5- 4- 3- 2- 1- and move. One moment of courage can change your day. One day can change your life. And your life can change the world.

There is greatness in you. The time to reveal it is now.

5...4...3...2...1...GO!

The 5 Second Rule

The moment you have an **instinct** to **act on a goal** you must

5-4-3-2-1

and **physically move** or your **brain will stop** you.